out for BLOOD

SUNY series, Praxis: Theory in Action

Nancy A. Naples, editor

out *for* BLOOD

essays on menstruation and resistance

Breanne Fahs

Front cover art: *The Menny Sides of Things, Series No. 6*, by Echo Thunderbolt
Back cover art: *Vicissitude*, by Sadie Mohler

Published by
STATE UNIVERSITY OF NEW YORK PRESS, ALBANY

For information, contact
State University of New York Press, Albany, NY
www.sunypress.edu

Production, Laurie D. Searl
Marketing, Fran Keneston

Library of Congress Cataloging-in-Publication Data

Names: Fahs, Breanne, author.
Title: Out for blood : essays on menstruation and resistance / Breanne Fahs.
Description: Albany : State University of New York Press, 2016. | Series:
   SUNY series, praxis: Theory in action | Includes bibliographical
   references and index.
Identifiers: LCCN 2016005972 | ISBN 9781438462134 (hardcover : alk.
   paper) | ISBN 9781438462127 (pbk. : alk. paper) | ISBN 9781438462141
   (e-book)
Subjects: LCSH: Menstruation. | Menstruation—Social aspects. |
   Menstruation—Public opinion.
Classification: LCC GN484.38 .F34 2016 | DDC 612.6/62—dc23
LC record available at https://lccn.loc.gov/2016005972

10 9 8 7 6 5 4 3 2 1

For my blood, Kristen (Fahs) Nusbaum,
and her blood, Ryan and Simon,
for reminding me just how deep and wild
the love of siblings can run

Contents

Part Four: Menarchy and Menstrual Activism

Introduction

On Dragons and Death Threats

Telling New Menstrual Stories

In 2012 Petra Collins, an outspoken artist and activist, designed a t-shirt for American Apparel that depicted a hairy menstruating vulva with fingers spreading open the labia. As a piece of agitprop, this shirt successfully provoked a firestorm of angry responses. Deemed "outrageous," "obscene," and "disgusting," with one news source calling it the "ultimate overshare," the shirt never reached the shelves but nevertheless stirred up a frenzied social media battle about gendered double standards of obscenity (Collins 2013). In 2015 artist Rupi Kaur posted several menstrual-themed photos on her Instagram account in an effort to demystify menstruation. These photos included one of her lying fully clothed with menstrual stains on her pants and sheets and another that showed her feet covered in dripping menstrual blood while she stood in the shower. Citing violations of community standards, Instagram twice removed the photographs and deemed them obscene (Saul 2015). Clearly, menstruation is not yet ready to come out of the menstrual closet, even in a culture that has supposedly dramatically improved gender inequities since the sexual revolution and women's movement of the 1970s.

Across the Pacific on the island of Komodo in Indonesia, menstrual conversations happen all the time and in the most public way imaginable, mostly to help women avoid being bitten by Komodo dragons. Because the dragons can smell blood (including menstrual blood) with remarkable accuracy and from great distances away—

causing them to aggressively pursue their targets—women who enter Komodo Island must sign waivers that attest to the fact that they are not currently menstruating; otherwise, government officials block them from entering the island altogether. These seemingly disparate anecdotes are but three of the many topics and stories about the contemporary culture of menstruation that *Out for Blood* examines.

Readers may ask, "Is there a *culture* of menstruation? A discourse of menstruation? Why does menstruation matter at all?" These questions form the basis of the necessary work that menstrual activists and scholars have taken up for many years. Half of the world's population menstruates for large periods of their lives and yet surprisingly little scholarship has addressed the social meanings around this experience, let alone its potential as a site of gendered resistance. While a small (and fierce) group of feminist social scientists has studied menstruation for decades, too often their contributions have ended up sidelined by mainstream psychology and sociology. Dismissed either as something secretive, hidden, and taboo (and therefore too threatening to openly discuss and analyze) or disregarded as trivial and "silly" (and therefore not worthy of serious attention), the culture around, and discourses about, menstruation remain largely undertheorized and underexamined. When I talk openly about writing a book about menstruation and menstrual activism, I often hear (after some expressions of discomfort and amusement) two responses: "What's that?" and "Why?"

What Is Menstrual Activism?

Menstrual activism—or social activism that works to upset, challenge, and reverse impulses to silence and shame menstruating women— has many goals, tactics, and styles. It takes as its central premise the fusion between menstruation and anarchy (some call menstrual activism "menarchy") and targets a wide range of social and political problems: the toxic substances in tampons and commercial menstrual products; increasing diagnoses of "premenstrual dysphoric disorder" (PMDD) and "premenstrual syndrome" (PMS); negative depictions of menstruating women in film, television, music, and popular culture; overmedicalization of menstrual cycles, including menstrual suppression; double standards in imagining women's bodies as "dirty" and men's bodies as "clean"; men's attitudes about menstruation and menstrual products; early menstrual education and messages of shame and taboo embedded in such messages; and a variety of other problematic aspects of contemporary menstrual culture.

Menstrual activism is both formal (e.g., Blood Sisters) and informal (e.g., individual women making menstrual art); it offers coherent, organized critiques and tactical interventions (e.g., working to pass a congressional bill on tampon safety), and it draws from organic and informal modes of communication and connection (e.g., women sharing first period stories on Facebook). It offers showy and artistic public displays (e.g., Spanish performance artists walking along public streets wearing pants stained with menstrual blood) and more private and subtle shifts of thinking (e.g., women embracing menstrual sex). It draws from the culture of punk and anarchy alongside the do-it-yourself aesthetic that arose in the early 1990s, just as it puts into dialogue diverse and sometimes painful social questions about bodies and identities. Chris Bobel (2010), whose work on menstrual activism stands out as exceptional, wrote of the possibilities of menstrual activism: "Menstrual activism helps us see what's at stake in the spirited debates about what to do about gender and the ongoing struggles to engage a truly racially, ethnically, and economically diverse movement of social change advocates around a common issue" (13). Menstrual activism offers multiple, diffuse, tactical, and intuitive forms of resistance, many of which this book considers in detail. It builds upon what we already know about the benefits of resistance, as those who rebel through activism on behalf of *any* issue have better physical health and more enjoyment of life (Rittenour and Colaner 2012), fewer eating disorders (Peterson, Grippo, and Tantleff-Dunn 2008), better mental health outcomes (Szymanski and Owens 2009), and more satisfying sex lives (Schick, Zucker, and Bay-Cheng 2008). I argue that *menstruation* and *resistance* go hand in hand, that menstruating bodies are always already infused with the potential for activism, solidarity, defiance, feminism, and rebellion.

Why Does Menstruation Matter?

With regard to *why* study menstrual activism and the culture of menstruation—in other words, why should we care?—my response typically gets more personal. While many people in the United States believe that sexism has almost disappeared in contemporary society (for a compelling critique of this rhetoric, see Swim and Cohen 1997), most researchers have identified uneven improvements in women's lives (Acker 2006; Bettie 2003). Paula England (2010) argues that the last twenty years have seen many improvements in gender inequities in the workplace, but the practices of people in their homes and personal lives have resisted change in ways that directly (and negatively) impact women's lives. Women's bodies and sexualities, in particular, continue to face assaults in terms of safety, well-being, body image, and pleasure (Armstrong and Hamilton 2013; Fahs 2011a). In the midst of this, menstruation continues to exist as a silenced, disregarded, and at times abject or "disgusting" aspect of women's daily lives. Negativity about menstruation subjects women to ridicule, dismissal, and trivialization (see Donald Trump's attack on Fox News anchor Megyn Kelly after the first presidential debate of 2015 in which he asserted that she asked him tough questions because she "had blood coming out of her eyes, blood coming out of her wherever").

I have long studied subjects that others have called trivial or foolish or unworthy of scholarly attention. Typically, these subjects include aspects of bodies—particularly women's bodies, bodies of color, and LGBT bodies—that connect to themes of agency/autonomy, social justice, and discourses of social control. For example, I have studied, written about, and taught about body hair for many years and have argued that hair is far from a trivial matter; rather, it symbolizes much about people's relationship to identity, beauty, power, gender, race, class, and notions of "choice" (Fahs 2011b; Fahs 2012a; Fahs 2013b; Fahs 2014). Similarly, menstruation, another subject too often labeled as trivial, also reflects much about our culture's relationship to women and their bodies, disgust, abjection, ideas about power and control, and gendered double standards (Fahs 2011c). The body is, I believe, an especially productive site of knowledge, and as such, serves as a serious point of analysis for those who want to understand the exercise, and deployment, of power.

In July 2014, I had the surreal experience of watching my work on body hair get taken up by the machine of the Far Right news media. After years of teaching an extra credit assignment where I asked students to grow out their body hair (women) or remove body hair (men) and write about the experience of engaging in nonnormative gendered body behavior, this assignment was "discovered" by conservatives and eventually discussed on air by both Rush Limbaugh and Fox News. I endured red- and feminist-baiting tropes and accusations of "ruining America" and being another Communist professor, and I received hundreds of pieces of hate mail claiming (at best) that I wasted parents' money on their children's education (notably assuming, of course, that parents pay for education, which is rarely true for my students who largely self-support their education, but I digress . . .) and that I demonstrated the failures and "idiocy" of women and gender studies. I also received hate mail calling me a Communist (and saying I ran a Communist training camp in my classrooms), a dyke, a whore, a (fat) bitch, and a cunt. (Clearly, the importance of studying vitriolic rhetoric about bodies and gender seemed ever more vivid to me during this experience, not to mention the painful links between homophobia and misogyny.)

As a result of this news coverage about my body hair assignment, I also received death threats. *Death threats.* Death threats because I wanted students to both think about, and actively engage with, discourses of body hair. I had to have a security team assess my personal safety (with some officials suggesting that the university install a "panic button" in my office), and I was suddenly immersed in emergency meetings, frantic phone calls, talks of patrolling my house for intruders, tech officials reading and analyzing my email for IP address patterns, revisions to my posted office hours, and new policies about student meetings and visiting faculty offices. Ironically, I also heard statements from top university officials reminding me that "this happens all the time to women faculty," but usually it derives from one or two stalkers rather than the far more public and diffuse audiences of Fox News and Rush Limbaugh. *This happens all the time?* Well, enough that my university employs a full-time person to handle threats made to faculty (largely, I heard, toward women faculty and faculty of color). In total, while I certainly also received plenty of heart-warming affirmations toward, and fan mail about, my work from colleagues both in the United States and abroad, the symbolic and literal *danger* of writing about and engaging students about issues of women's bodies became foregrounded to me in new and important ways.

Telling New Menstrual Stories

Returning to the question, then, of why menstruation matters—and how women's bodies inspire panic when not behaving in gender-normative, predictable, socially controlled ways—I argue in this book that we *must* take menstruation seriously. Menstruation provides the perfect platform through which to examine the synthesis of serious things: political identities (feminism, antiracism, queer subjectivities), body consciousness/knowledge, gender issues and identities, the insidious aspects of inequalities, and the possibilities inherent in activism and resistance. These themes weave in and out of the topics discussed in *Out for Blood*, particularly how people talk about menstruation (in therapy, in popular culture, with their partners), how menstruation is appropriated and distorted, various assumptions about menstrual distress, moral panics about menstrual blood, notions of menstrual contagions, the value of alternative menstrual products, menstrual art, and, most notably, the ongoing work of menstrual activists fighting to release menstruation from the jaws of capitalism and patriarchy. Further, menstruation represents a way for women (and menstruating men) to possibly have shared language, bodily connection, and perhaps even some solidarity with each other—all of which are in remarkably short supply today.

To achieve these liberatory goals, we need new menstrual stories, ones that adequately capture the ways that seemingly ordinary processes of the body can have extraordinary implications for social justice movements. How people resist the silenced and secretive discourse of menstruation opens up new ways to approach, think about, study, and manage (or not) menstrual cycles. In these essays, I question the phrase *feminine hygiene*, interrogate misperceptions about how much women bleed, showcase the conflicts of the menstruating male body and trans experiences of menstruation, turn an eye toward the global landscape of menstruation and resistance work abroad, and ask us to contemplate fantasies of rebellion. Here, too, menstruation becomes a litmus test, a metaphor, an intuitive "cousin" to other body and identity practices and questions such as body hair, queer identity, pregnancy and childbirth, sexuality, trans politics, and radical feminism.

Out for Blood asks a variety of important questions that have immediate relevance to contemporary studies of the body and menstruation: What do contemporary discourses of menstruation say, or not say, about the menstruating body, and how might these discourses expand or change over time? How does menstrual solidarity speak to larger questions of political activism and feminist collectivism? How do menstrual anarchists resist, and what can their work teach us about our own bodies and the knowledges of the body? In what ways do our current tools and products for managing, tracking, and controlling menstrual cycles reveal particular assumptions about gender, sexuality, and power? How do women discuss their menstrual cycles in therapy, in the classroom, at home, and in public, and what does this show about the various modes of containment and expression that menstruation engenders? Why is menstrual discourse relevant to men, and what can trans men teach us about menstruation? How can the disgusting or abject qualities of menstruation signify new modes of understanding gender and the body? Finally, how can people learn and unlearn knowledge about menstrual cycles, and how can they fight back, resist, and reconstruct new menstrual stories both individually and collectively?

Overview

Designed to move across multiple discursive spaces and modalities, this book features eleven essays divided into four distinct sections, with six longer essays and five shorter essays comprising the collection. Meant as a lively interdisciplinary interrogation about the contemporary culture of menstruation—sometimes more formally, sometimes less formally—the book moves through feminist theory, social science, psychotherapy discourses, cultural studies, trans studies, sexuality studies, and gender studies. These four parts include: Part One: Theorizing Cycles and Stains, two longer essays designed to connect menstruation to feminist theory; Part Two: Dispatches from the Blogosphere, five shorter essays targeting the relationship between menstruation and cultural stories/discourses; Part Three: Blood on the Couch, two longer essays about how psychotherapy clients talk about their menstrual cycles; and Part Four: Menarchy and Menstrual Resistance, two longer essays about menstrual activists and forms of resistance.

Part One: Theorizing Cycles and Stains

I begin the book with two essays that fuse feminist theory with the study of menstruation. Chapter 1 ("Cycling Together: Menstrual Synchrony as a Projection of Gendered Solidarity") draws upon controversial literatures on the biological theories of menstrual synchrony—that is, the notion that menstruating women living in proximity eventually sync up over time—in order to analyze the reasons why women *want* to believe that they cycle together. I argue that women's beliefs in menstrual synchrony function as a projection of gendered solidarity whereby they can create social ties and social bonds with women in spaces that largely prohibit such alliances. This essay draws from sociological theories of collectivism and political solidarity, biological and evolutionary science, and from feminist theories of "affective solidarity" to explore menstrual synchrony and its social and political implications.

Chapter 2 ("The Menstrual Stain as Graffiti") uses Julia Kristeva's classic philosophical text, *Powers of Horror*, to interrogate the meaning of the menstrual stain in relation to the abject. The essay looks at how the browning, decaying, provocatively gendered symbol of the menstrual stain ("blood-turned-to-death") threatens to elicit panicky reactions by functioning not only as a material symbol of death but also as a highly gendered form of graffiti that attaches death to the decaying, feminine, female body. The essay asks: How does the process of "bleeding through," of using the menstrual stain to (unwittingly) leave a mark, provoke and disrupt boundaries, borders, and bodily order? Further, what sorts of feminist resistances can be imagined in and through the menstrual stain as a transgressive representation of the abject?

Part Two: Dispatches from the Blogosphere

The second section of the book includes five short essays derived from my work on the menstrual blog *Re:Cycling*. These pieces are designed as brief, sometimes provocative and controversial, and often politicized pieces about a range of topics related to menstrual culture and discourse today. Chapter 3 ("In Praise of Cycles") posits that capitalism and contemporary norms and practices of people's work lives have largely destroyed the intuitive and positive understandings of cycles, particularly with regard to the body, mood, seasons, and cycles of work. Chapter 4 ("'Feminine Hygiene' and the Ultimate Double Standard") unpacks the history of the phrase *feminine hygiene* and its implications for women's bodies as dirty or in need of management.

Building on these essays, chapter 5 ("Adventures on Komodo Island") recounts my story of visiting Komodo Island, Indonesia, where women must declare their menstrual status to government officials before entering the island. The chapter examines not only the cultural conversations around menstruation in this part of Indonesia but also explores the implications of having such public conversations with my group of travelers from Australia, the United States, and the United Kingdom.

The final two essays in this section address themes of menstruation, technology, and history. Chapter 6 ("Menstruation according to Apple") provides a critical look at recent technology that tracks menstrual periods and the various assumptions embedded within these apps (e.g., pregnancy as good, periods as inherently distressing). Finally, chapter 7 ("Collateral Damage: Throwing Menstruation Out of the Museum") examines the way that coming-of-age narratives in a museum dedicated to Native American cultures have largely ignored menstruation even while other rituals and bodily practices garner attention. This chapter questions the various stories associated with menstruating girls and women and how our menstrual coming-of-age stories are obscured by political and artistic claims of "decency" and "obscenity."

Part Three: Blood on the Couch

Part 3 emphasizes the unique intersection between menstruation and psychotherapy by drawing on a series of case studies with former clients. Chapter 8 ("Blood on the Couch: Disclosures about Menstruation in the Therapy Room") focuses on disclosures about menstruation from three different female patients in order to explore how menstruation functions as a taboo, a mode of alliance with the therapist, an expression of personal distress, and a way to understand more salient problems with family members and body image. Ultimately, I argue in this chapter that women experience strongly paradoxical feelings about their menstrual cycles, seeing them on the one hand as a source of intense distress and, on the other, as a site of resistance and emotional expression. Chapter 9 ("The Menstruating Male Body") draws from my work with three female-to-male (FTM) trans men in therapy who discuss their menstrual cycles and the various stressors and traumas of menstruating. Unworking notions of male and female bodies, questioning the inherent meanings and symbolism of menstruation, and working toward seeing menstruation as potentially masculine or genderqueer all helped to underscore the power of menstruation to make and remake gender.

Part Four: Menarchy and Menstrual Activism

I end the book with two essays that explore the work of contemporary menstrual activists and the ways that they fight back against shame-based menstrual culture, inspire new thinking about menstruating bodies, and reimagine individual and collective efforts to engage in menstrual anarchy. Chapter 10 ("Raising Bloody Hell: Inciting Menstrual Panics through Campus and Community Activism") features the work of undergraduate menstrual activists and the various menstrual panics they incited for the Arizona politicians who found their work "obscene." The chapter highlights the role of seemingly simple acts of rebellion—for example, raising awareness about the toxicity of tampons, asking drivers to "honk if you love menstrual sex"—and their far-reaching consequences and implications. Chapter 11 ("Smear It on Your Face: Menstrual Art, Performance, and Zines as Menstrual Activism") features the work of menstrual artists, public menstrual stunts, and menstrual zines to outline a future vision for menarchy, including new spaces for menstrual activists to invade, new projects to undertake, and new ways to move menstruation out of the "menstrual closet." This chapter concludes the book with a playful romp through the performative fantasy and hyper-reality of menstruation today.

Ultimately, this book of essays aims to provoke discussion about how to cultivate and circulate new menstrual stories, ones that affirm menstruation as a complicated, potentially powerful, sometimes distressing, always provocative space of self-understanding and collective meaning-making. By asking new questions ("How do people talk about menstruation with their female therapists?" or "What assumptions underlie the design of period tracker apps?") and featuring new voices (e.g., zine writers, European menstrual activists, artists using menstrual blood in their work, Komodo Island government officials), the cultures and discourses of menstruation become more vivid, rich, and varied. Further, links between the body and the tactical deployment of power (and resistance to that power) appear in poignant ways when studying menstruation, making it all the more urgent and compelling as an entry point into practices that cultivate social justice. The study of the body is necessarily messy; I hope we can collectively revel in that messiness, find new ways to understand ourselves and each other, and attach the experiences of our bodies to a fierce and shameless politics of resistance, rebellion, and revolution.

Part One

Theorizing Cycles and Stains

1

Cycling Together

Menstrual Synchrony as a
Projection of Gendered Solidarity

In 1971, a time when the U.S. women's movement had catalyzed women to see themselves as aligned and in political solidarity with other women, Martha McClintock published a study on menstrual synchrony among college women living in a shared dormitory. McClintock's study—the first of its kind and one that would go on to inspire decades of additional research in this area—of 135 women ages seventeen to twenty-two living together yielded statistically significant levels of menstrual synchrony among pairs of friends and groups of female friends. The results of her study, quickly picked up by the media, spread rapidly throughout the scientific and lay communities, appearing as a fact presented on television (Rosewarne 2012) and a hotly disputed occurrence within the scientific literature (McClintock 1971, 1998; Schank 2000, 2001; Strassmann 1999; Weller and Weller 1992, 1993a, 1993b, 1995a, 1995b, 1998; Weller, Weller, and Avinir 1995; Weller, Weller, and Roizman 1999).

Here, we are less interested in the scientific debates about the existence of menstrual synchrony—though the literature itself is a fascinating example of the controversies of science followed by an ultimate lack of conclusiveness—and more interested in the personal, social, and political implications of *why many women believe they have menstrual synchrony with other women.* In line with the feminist call to fuse the personal and political, the theoretical positions presented in this chapter are derived from our work as menstrual activists. As we have challenged and sought to combat the shame-based, sexist, and menstrual-negative culture around us, we have had ample opportunities to engage in conversations with women about menstruation, which has provided us a unique lens through which to view the political meanings of menstrual synchrony. Through casual conversations about menstruation on airplanes; dialogue with family, friends, students, and coworkers; workshops about alternative menstrual products; and discussions about menstrual cycles during psychotherapy, we have been continually curious about the frequency with which we have heard the statement: *I menstruate together with my sister/friends/mother/ coworkers/lover.*

Struck by the consistency, passion, and certainty that women have when describing menstrual synchrony, particularly given that those on hormonal contraceptives do not actually menstruate, we see the overwhelming presence of the belief in menstrual synchrony as a projection of gendered solidarity with other women. Specifically, we posit at least four different possible functions of menstrual synchrony: a way to reduce shame and taboo related to menstruation; a socially acceptable way of constructing modern "sisterhood"; a method for marking women's relationship to nature; and a pathway to fight back against sexism and sexist assumptions about menstruation and menstruating women. All of these functions underlie the importance of seeing solidarity not only on purely *political* terms but also as a *bodily, gendered, and largely personal phenomenon* that has the potential to create, validate, and perpetuate social bonds between women.

Debates about Menstrual Synchrony

The menstrual synchrony literature is an unusual, controversial, and passionate literature filled with rebuttals, conflicted opinions, backtracking, accusations of methodological error, and passionate defensiveness. When we reviewed the literature on menstrual synchrony, we were reminded of Elizabeth Lloyd's (2006) brilliant work in which she examined the biases of science and the ways that scientists projected their beliefs about gender and sexuality onto their evolutionary studies of orgasm. In essence, Lloyd found that, despite having no conclusive evolutionary purpose whatsoever, many scientists nevertheless reported as fact that the female orgasm has a reproductive purpose. Even in the face of contradictory evidence, researchers, blinded by their own attitudes toward and beliefs about women and sex, proceeded to argue "facts" that ultimately had no scientific basis. How researchers see—and what they see—leans heavily on their desires for what they *want* to see, even (or especially) within the supposedly neutral and bias-free scientific community.

The literature on menstrual synchrony has many unusual qualities, as its origin date, size, lack of conclusiveness, and large volume of repeated follow-up studies suggest that the *idea* of menstrual synchrony tapped into something much larger than the mere possibility of menstrual cycle alignment. The number of studies that followed McClintock's (1971) pioneering work helped to describe how women living together might menstruate together. McClintock, a psychologist at the University of Chicago who has studied human pheromones, menstrual synchrony, and the behavioral control of endocrinology, brought a distinctly feminist lens to the study of women's health and menstrual synchrony. Her most vocal critics (and those who have wavered back and forth about the existence of menstrual synchrony) have included J. C. Schank, a male psychologist who focuses on animal behavior and biopsychology; Leonard Weller, a sociologist who has studied social class and anti-Semitism (with a clear interest in social relationships between people); and Aron Weller, a psychologist interested in neuropsychology and animal behavior. Collectively, these four researchers have spent much of their careers debating the existence of menstrual synchrony and attempting to have the "final word" on the matter; it is important to note that some of them are primarily interested in animal behavior and not in health-related matters.

Theoretical Debates

Following McClintock's (1971) landmark study, other researchers examined a variety of contexts where women cohabitated or existed in close proximity, including lesbian couples (Trevathan, Burleson, and Gregory 1993; Weller and Weller 1992), friends and roommates (Graham and McGrew 1980; Jarett 1984; Weller and Weller 1993a; Weller, Weller, and Avinir 1995; Wilson, Kiefhaber, and Gravel 1991), sisters and mothers/daughters (Weller, Weller, and Roizman 1999), coworkers (Matteo 1987; Weller and Weller 1995b; Weller et al. 1999), athletes (Weller and Weller 1995a), and women not using any birth control (Collett, Wertenberger, and Fiske 1955; Strassmann 1997). Some studies found synchrony between roommates and friends but not mothers (Weller and Weller 1993b) and that closer friendships developed more menstrual synchrony (Weller and Weller 1995b), whereas others found a large variety of factors related to menstrual synchrony, including social factors, quality of the relationships, group size, age and age diversity, menstrual regularity, the environment, and contraceptive practices (Little et al. 1989; Weller and Weller 1995c; Weller and Weller 1997). However, researchers have not assessed menstrual synchrony in groups of women who all use hormonal birth control, and some rightly note that this sort of withdrawal bleeding is different from menstruation altogether (for two studies that excluded women on birth control, see Preti et al. 1986; Russell, Switz, and Thompson 1980).

Pheromone studies have formed the basis of much of the research on menstrual synchrony to date. Although friendship, common activities, cohabitating, and the amount of time spent together all correlated with higher reports of menstrual synchrony, the researchers believed that exposure to other women's ovarian-based pheromones (i.e., odorless compounds emitted from women's bodies, especially their underarms) was largely responsible for why women cycled together (Goldman and Schneider 1987; Weller and Weller 1993a). The release of these pheromones was assumed to accelerate or delay the surge of luteinizing hormone responsible for menstrual cycle length, which resulted in women becoming increasingly more synchronized with each other (Stern and McClintock 1998).

Though many studies consistently demonstrated the existence of menstrual synchrony (particularly those by Weller and Weller), one study showed that it occurred only because of environmental influences (Little et al. 1989), and results of a number of studies led researchers to question its existence or refute its existence entirely (Jarrett 1984; Schank 2002; Strassmann 1999; Trevathan, Burleson, and Gregory 1993; Weller and Weller 1998; Weller, Weller, and Avinir 1995; Wilson, Kiefhaber, and Gravel 1991; Yang and Schank 2006; Ziomkiewicz 2006). Wilson (1992) showed that, mathematically, menstrual synchrony would be expected in half of the women studied without any external manipulation or contextual factors influencing it, as some women cycle regularly and some irregularly. He also found three methodological errors that could have skewed the results of earlier studies: too short an observational period, incorrect methods of calculating the menstrual onset differences, and exclusion of certain women from the analysis.

Evolutionary biologists have also debated the existence of menstrual synchrony, as strong disagreements appear in the literature as to whether (and why) menstrual synchrony occurs (McClintock 1998). Evolutionary scientists have theorized a variety of reasons for menstrual synchrony, including the higher likelihood for conception in societies where many women share one man (he would sense the pheromones, want to have sex with multiple women, and impregnation would become more likely, whereas unsynchronized cycles would "confuse" men) (Burley 1979). Menstrual synchrony has also been proposed to increase a man's interest in his female offspring (Knowlton 1979; Turke 1984) or provide a backup wet nurse in times of high maternal mortality (Frisch 1984).

Despite these evolutionary explanations, no studies have shown that women ovulate together or have similar fertility periods while cohabitating, which refutes the likelihood of most of the evolutionary explanations (Kiltie 1982; Strassmann 1999; Yang and Schank 2006; Ziomkiewicz 2006). Even more important, urbanized and nonurbanized societies show markedly different patterns of fertility and menstruation, as women in urbanized societies have more menstrual cycles, fewer pregnancies (and longer periods of nursing), and more years when they menstruate than do women in nonurbanized societies (Strassmann 1997; Strassmann 1999; Umeora and Egwuatu 2008). Some recent evolutionary researchers have cautioned that scientists know very little about menstrual synchrony and its possible reasons, and, consequently, researchers should not draw sweeping conclusions about such a complex phenomenon (Harris and Vitzthum 2013).

Methodological Debates

Several researchers have found additional methodological problems, particularly the difficulty of assessing menstrual synchrony in light of "within" and "between" women differences. Each individual woman may not have a consistent cycle length (e.g., Woman A has a 28-day cycle in one month and a 31-day cycle in another), just as women often differ between one another in their average cycle lengths (Woman

A typically has 28-day cycles, and Woman B typically has 31-day cycles) (Schank 2000). Finally, some researchers found no evidence of menstrual synchrony among those not using hormonal contraceptives (Strassmann 1997; Strassmann 1999), and a few studies yielded no evidence of menstrual synchrony in lesbian couples (Trevathan, Burleson, and Gregory 1993; Weller and Weller 1998), which called into doubt the existence of menstrual synchrony in its entirety.

Furthermore, the methodological problems of studying menstrual synchrony—particularly Weller and Weller's methods—may have *created* the phenomenon as an artifact of how it was studied (Schank 2000). In his review of all studies of menstrual synchrony, Schank (2001) concluded that allowing women to fill out their own menstrual onset calendars may have encouraged women to *want* to report synchrony rather than their actual onset dates. Weller and Weller wrote two rebuttal pieces, in which they asserted that they had used sound methods (Weller and Weller 2002a, 2002b), and Schank (2002) replied that Weller and Weller over-relied upon recall data. In short, women who *wanted to have menstrual synchrony may have remembered and reported menstrual synchrony.* He then went on to show that no evidence of menstrual synchrony existed (Yang and Schank 2006) and that all eight of the pheromone studies had "serious problems" with methodological errors (Schank 2006).

Subjective Feelings about Menstrual Synchrony

Debates among biological researchers have dominated the menstrual synchrony literature, but a few social scientists have measured women's subjective feelings about their personal experiences of menstrual synchrony. One qualitative study of thirteen white highly educated women, ages twenty-five to forty-six, showed that *all* of the women reported having experienced menstrual synchrony, and most thought that there were biological rather than social reasons for its occurrence (e.g., about hormones or chemicals) (Klebanoff and Keyser 1996). Another study (Arden, Dye, and Walker 1999) showed that women overwhelmingly knew about menstrual synchrony and believed that they had experienced it. In this study of 122 British women, 84 percent were aware of menstrual synchrony (note that the authors did not present menstrual synchrony as a controversy), and 70 percent reported personal experiences with it (Arden, Dye, and Walker 1999). Further, the women reported having experienced synchrony with close friends, roommates, mothers, and sisters, and 51 percent of them reported three or more episodes of synchrony with different women. The women in this study felt positively about menstrual synchrony (e.g., supportive, closeness, mysticism), and they said they knew about the timing of other women's menstrual cycles primarily through verbal communication and complaints about PMS symptoms.

The Media Storm about Menstruating Together

This critique that women may *want* to report menstrual synchrony and that their desire to experience it potentially biased the findings in Weller and Weller's work seems highly plausible given the volume of interest in and unequivocal belief in menstrual synchrony displayed in popular culture. Most film and television sources have not portrayed menstrual synchrony as a controversy. From women's magazines to television shows to blogs (Clancy 2011; Rosewarne 2012), women hear (and likely internalize) the notion that women who live together bleed together. As Rosewarne (2012) wrote in her analysis of the presentation of menstrual synchrony on television: "The menstrual synchrony narrative is perhaps the strongest example of on-screen menstrual bonding, presenting women not merely united by menstruation, but by the experience of bleeding *simultaneously*" (20).

Television shows and films have sometimes depicted menstrual synchrony both as a bond between women and as a source of horror. The series *Charmed* (1998–2006) depicted three witches with aligned periods: Phoebe (Alyssa Milano) was more "emotional," Paige (Rose McGowan) was more "jumpy," and Piper (Holly Marie Combs) was more "pissy." In an episode of *30 Rock*, Jack (Alec Baldwin) remarked offhandedly, "Oh sure, we can sit around and braid each other's hair until we get our periods at the same time." Howard (Simon Helberg) in *The Big Bang Theory* joked after watching *Sex and the City*: "Fine, let's watch it. Maybe all our periods will synchronize." And, on *The Office* (2005–2013), Dwight (Rainn Wilson) sarcastically advised against women meeting together on their own: "If they stay in there too long, they're gonna get on the same cycle. Wreak havoc on our plumbing." An example of the "horrors" of menstrual synchrony is found in the Korean film *A Tale of Two Sisters* (2013), which displayed two sisters who awoke to realize they were menstruating together— something the film portrays as weird and otherworldly (Rosewarne 2012).

Women's magazines and blogs also offer a host of (mis)information about menstrual synchrony, such as that menstrual synchrony is based on exposure to natural light (MacLeod 2013) and that menstrual cycle–related pheromones determine the likelihood of conception (Edmonds 2010). Magazines such as *Women's Health, Shape, Women's Day, New Scientist,* and *Bust* have all discussed menstrual synchrony as well, sometimes presenting it as a compelling controversy but most often describing it as a real phenomenon. *Shape* writers leaned heavily on the argument that women have menstrual synchrony: "And it's hard to say how factors like stress, sexual partners, and birth control play into the syncing game—if synchrony does exist, it's possible these factors override it, making matched cycles appear less common than they might actually be" (Newcomer 2012). Dozens of blogs—feminist, scientific, health, and personal—have discussed menstrual synchrony, usually portraying it as a common and everyday occurrence.

Menstrual Solidarity

Given this evidence, particularly that scientific research has never conclusively determined that menstrual synchrony actually exists and that the media nevertheless has taken it up largely as factual, we consider the concept of "menstrual solidarity" to be a key motivator for maintaining the story of menstrual synchrony. We now propose our theories about *why women believe in menstrual synchrony.*

The concept of feminist or gendered solidarity has most often been used as a political and moral concept, that is, fighting for members of one's own groups and communities in the *public sphere* (Mohanty 2003), such as social movements against war, collective bargaining, protests against policies, and group actions against the powers of the state. However, solidarity can also involve linkages and connections in private spheres, including women's reproductive health. Politicized collective identities often require an awareness of shared grievances, adversarial attributions, and involvement in society at large (Simon and Klandermans 2001); thus, menstrual solidarity may work as a way to address, on a highly personal level, an awareness of shared grievances and may, in some cases, allow women to work toward identifying an adversary (e.g., sexism) and becoming involved in society at large (e.g., activism) via their reproductive health.

Some sociologists have conceptualized these linkages as *frame transformation*, that is, the process by which something negative transforms in meaning and becomes the basis for political activism and solidarity (Snow et al. 1986). In this case, menstrual solidarity may function to transform menstruation from a shameful or taboo experience into something more positive. Some feminist theorists have called for a radical reenvisioning of feminist solidarity, arguing for *affective* solidarity based on emotions rather than identities (Hemmings 2012), a deeper analysis of how women relate to each other in the face of patriarchal power (Cornwall 2007), and/or a reinvention of the collective, multifaceted sense of "we" (Dean 1997). In addition, feminist social scientists have addressed the importance of women's collectivism (Gurin, Miller, and Gurin 1980), menstrual anarchy and menstrual activism (Bobel 2006; Bobel 2010; Fahs 2013a), and how stories of menarche (girls' first periods) can connect people to larger cultural, religious, and societal stories that concern women (Uskul 2004) and give girls a greater sense of solidarity with other girls and women (Jackson and Falmagne 2013; Lee 1994). In light of this, we take seriously the questions of how one's community and in-groups are constructed, particularly in connection to menstruation, and how women have specifically faced barriers to conceptualizing themselves as a part of women-only communities.

Radical feminists of the late 1960s conceptualized women's solidarity as both a necessity in the fight against patriarchy and as quite difficult in light of family and living arrangements that presumably separate women and pair them with men. Radical feminists like Boston's Cell 16, New York Radical Women, and Redstockings argued for the value of "women only spaces," celibacy-by-choice, and even political lesbianism (Atkinson 1974; Dunbar 1974; Dworkin 1989; Sarachild 1975; Solanas 1996), and they fought for recognition that women's shared sexual, political, domestic, social, and personal experiences with other women could all form the basis for dramatic political changes. And, in many ways, these spaces did create numerous advances that have since eroded or been lost with the abandonment of women-only communities and politically based separation from men. Radical feminists fought for abortion rights (Koedt, Levine, and Rapone 1973), rape crisis centers, domestic violence shelters, better health care for women, and women-only spaces for political organizing and solidarity, just as they took a firmly critical stance against heterosexual marriage and child rearing (Echols 1989; Frye 1983). At the core of their assertions stood a unique definition of solidarity: Because women so rarely have opportunities to prioritize their "woman-identified" experiences and spaces, solidarity must be *created* and *recognized* by seeing women *as a class* (Atkinson 1974).

Theorizing the Belief in Menstrual Solidarity

After collectively working through the possible reasons for an insistence on menstrual solidarity, we theorize that the belief in menstrual synchrony serves a variety of purposes, each of which sheds light on why women may *want* to believe in menstrual solidarity. We propose that menstrual synchrony serves as: 1) a way to reduce shame and taboo narratives related to menstruation; 2) a socially acceptable way of constructing modern "sisterhood"; 3) a method for reinforcing connections between women, their bodies, and nature; and 4) a pathway to fight back against sexism and sexist assumptions about menstruation and menstruating women. To illustrate these themes, we give examples from our menstrual activist work alongside our collective theorizing about what might underlie claims of menstrual solidarity.

Reducing Shame and Taboo Related to Menstruation

Silence, shame, and taboos related to menstruation have defined women's menstrual cycles for many generations. To consider why menstrual solidarity may be so appealing to U.S. women, the context of menstrual negativity must be assessed. When women worry about their menstrual cycles, or see their menstrual periods as "dirty" or "disgusting," they are reflecting a long history of revulsion regarding menstruation and women's bodies. Historically, women learned to see menstruation as taboo and as something in need of management (Delaney, Lupton, and Toth 1988); in various cultures and times, menstrual blood has signified disease, corruption, social violations (Read 2008; Shuttle and Redgrove 1988), failed reproduction (Kerkham 2003; Martin 2001), and disability (Kissling 2006). Women face an onslaught of negative imagery about menstruation, as the media implies that menstruation makes women "unclean" (Briefel 2005; Kissling 2006; Rosewarne 2012), and the medicalization of menstruation has resulted in women seeing their menstrual cycles as inconvenient, unnecessary, something to medicate away, and, in the worst cases, something that causes mental illness (Johnston-Robledo, Barnack, and Wares 2006; Rose, Chrisler, and Couture 2008). Advertisers routinely depict women's menstruating bodies as unfeminine, dirty, tainted, and disgusting in order to sell pads, panty liners, and tampons to consumers (Berg and Coutts 1994; Davidson 2012; Kissling 2006). Even the phrase *feminine hygiene*, a relic from 1930s advertisements for birth control, connotes that women should construct menstrual blood as fundamentally dirty (Tone 1996).

Though women may not always recognize their collective status as women, they do face collective struggles, such as menstrual negativity and the shaming of women's bodies. In fact, women and girls in the United States typically face a lifetime of negative messages about menstruation. Girls learn early on to dislike their menstruating bodies, and this attitude has been found most pervasively among older girls (Rembeck, Moller, and Gunnarsson 2006), those prone to self-objectification (Roberts and Waters 2004), those with less sexual experience and more body shame (Schooler et al. 2005), and those who communicated with their mothers less frequently about menstruation (Rembeck, Moller, and Gunnarsson 2006). As adults, links between menstrual negativity and shame regarding breastfeeding (Johnston-Robledo et al. 2007) also appear. Further, women often internalize the idea that sex during menstruation is "dirty," "disgusting," and "gross." In one study, less than one half of the women said they had ever engaged in menstrual sex, and over 30 percent said that they would *never* do so (Allen and Goldberg 2009). In another study, heterosexual women reported far more negative feelings about menstrual sex than did lesbians or bisexual women (even if they had male partners) (Fahs 2011c).

Given this history, it makes sense that women generally approach menstruation from a position of silence and shame, as they manage their menses quietly and efficiently and rarely discuss anything about menstruation publicly. As menstrual activists, when we approach people to discuss menstruation—even the relatively benign topic of alternative menstrual products—these conversations are often met with disdain and discomfort (e.g., nervously changing the subject). The notable exception, however, is when women describe menstrual synchrony. Claims of menstrual solidarity, we theorize, function as a way to fight back against the silence and secrecy that surrounds menstruation, as menstrual synchrony provides one of the only socially acceptable *positive* attributes women can openly discuss about menstruation. Further, they can discuss the actual *bleeding* that occurs during menstruation; this is rarely discussed publicly or collectively otherwise.

Menstrual synchrony also provides an in-road for women to discuss menstruation in nonpathologizing language. Women would rarely say things like "I bled through my pants today. How are you?" or "I'm passing some large clots right now," whereas they *will* say, "My friend and I cycle together." This comment opens conversation and allows the topic of menstruation to exist without being framed entirely as a negative or disgusting experience. In short, women can take a break from the process of self-loathing so common in menstrual discourse and instead embrace *affective solidarity* (Hemmings 2012).

A Socially Acceptable Way of Constructing Modern "Sisterhood"

At the onset of the women's movement in the late 1960s, discussions of "sisterhood" permeated the political and social fabric of the budding feminist scene. The concept of "sisterhood" originated in the Middle Ages to describe groups of nuns living together (Ludlow 1866); the women's movement, however, saw this phrase as an opportunity to establish political bonds between women (Morgan 1970, 1984). Feminists in the late 1960s and early 1970s used sisterhood as a bridge to connect women from different social backgrounds, create stories of shared histories and experiences, and cultivate consciousness-raising about injustices they faced at home (Morgan 1970). As the years passed, these notions of "sisterhood" created during the women's movement largely dropped away. Consciousness-raising groups—once used as early women's studies curricula and widely popular with women from diverse backgrounds (Kravetz, Marecek, and Finn 1983)— no longer occur with any regularity, and sisterhood has largely been appropriated by consumer culture and capitalism to drive up sales on "girlie" items (e.g., Spice Girls music, Barbie dolls, *Sisterhood of the Traveling Pants*). The tradition of sisterhood has been taken up in postfeminist discourses as a way to celebrate girlhood and girl power through an antifeminist lens that reaffirms traditional patriarchal values about women (Bae 2011). Furthermore, one study of media consumption showed that adult women enjoy teen television shows, such as *Charmed*, because they often include themes of sisterhood, which shows how the media taps into sisterhood as a commodity that can be sold to specific audiences (Feasey 2006).

Menstrual synchrony, it seems, may serve as a somewhat socially acceptable way to (re)claim a space for "sisterhood." Indications of our shared experience with other women (e.g., we *menstruate together*) realign us with the notion that women as a group are connected, that we share common experiences, and that we cope with (or, in fewer cases, celebrate) our menstrual cycles. Unlike other common experiences for women (e.g., breastfeeding, pregnancy, careers, child rearing), menstrual cycles signal a nearly universal experience for adult women across all demographics. Based on sociological frameworks for collective identity (Ashmore, Deaux, and McLaughlin-Volpe 2004), we believe that menstrual solidarity may function as a way both to attach ourselves to other women and to claim a sense of interdependence with other women. After all, menstrual synchrony implies that *my cycle is dependent on yours.* Theoretically, then, women may be able to see this and other aspects of their lives as connected to, and dependent on, other women's lives—a rare opportunity to reinforce women's interdependence at the exclusion of men.

This sense of connection to other women may also appear in women's shared accounts of menstrual misery, as premenstrual syndrome (PMS) and premenstrual dysphoric disorder (PMDD) create a context for women to assess negative symptoms of their menstrual cycles in a collective way. As research has shown that women identify PMS symptoms as a common way to communicate about their menstrual cycles (Arden, Dye, and Walker 1999), sisterhood may appear as a shared expression of feeling bloated, crampy, or irritable. We have even seen this within our own research group, as we have sometimes expressed in the meetings that we are bleeding heavily or have strong cramps. Dunnavant and Roberts (2013) found that women of "prescriptive religions" (i.e., religions that emphasize religious authority figures as a conduit through which to speak with their higher power) often had a sense of community with other menstruating women;

when these religions dictated certain rituals or actions around men-struation, women sometimes benefited from them (e.g., worshipping together). Because of the strict prohibitions within certain religions, women found that "menarche becomes a time to welcome girls into a community of menstruating women who will go on to teach them the prescriptions and prohibitions specific to their culture" (127).

Although these sorts of connections based on menstruation may seem less ideal than a positive identification between women based on shared experiences and goals, distress (and, ideally, the *recognition of* women's collective distress) has been a basis for much political organizing and solidarity work (Hemmings 2012; Mohanty 2003). Perhaps the identification of individual symptoms and experiences with menstruation—however troubling in light of the overmedicaliza-tion of women's bodies (Chrisler 2011)—can underlie women's social and political bonds.

Women Marking Their Relationship to Nature

Women also may claim menstrual synchrony as a way to demarcate the unique links between women, lunar cycles, nature, and their bodies. Although connections between women and animals (Harris and Vitzthum 2013), and women and their bodies (Martin 2001), have been fraught with political tensions about whether these links reinforce oppression or solidify bonds between women, menstrual solidarity can serve as a women-only space to resist patriarchal power. In other words, although links between women and animals/nature play directly into dangerous dichotomies between (masculine) rationality and (feminine) irrationality, or between (masculine) unemotionality and (feminine) emotionality, these overlaps also serve as potentially separatist and politically charged. We argue that if women openly discuss menstruation, particularly how they menstruate *together*, the discussion allows female-bodied people to mark a mystical, unique, perhaps even sacred relationship to nature (and each other) that male-bodied people simply lack. Such conversations also directly confront notions of menstruation as frankly abject and terrifying by pushing against menstruation as a symbol of death (Kristeva 1982).

When women articulate menstrual synchrony and mark their relationship to nature, we believe that they are fostering a sense of power that has been taken away from them because of patriarchy, urbanization, medicalization, capitalism, and an overvaluing of so-called "masculine" life. For example, the general distaste that both patriarchy and capitalism have for cycles—the denial of cycles altogether, the lack of varied work schedules, the need for constant twenty-four seven production, excessive emphasis on work at the expense of leisure, and so on—is abundant throughout most people's lives (Martin 2001). By claiming menstrual solidarity and establishing their connections to nature, women are also resisting sexist forces, valuing their cyclic life, and reclaiming their relationship to lunar cycles and to the natural world.

As a vivid story that depicts this process, one of us who has regularly lived among anarchists and feminists in communal living environments has repeatedly heard discussions not only of menstrual synchrony but of lunar synchrony ("What moon phase do you cycle with?"). These conversations have allowed women to create bonds without having to include men and to situate their bodies cycling together as a positive aspect of their lives. Menstrual conversations— and overlaps women find in their menstrual experiences—have functioned to solidify political and affective alliances between women in these already radical communities as well as allowed women to identify their links to nature and lunar cycling.

A Pathway to Fight Back against Sexism and Sexist Assumptions about Menstruation

Sociologists have framed collective identity as people's belief that they have "a place in the social world" (Simon and Klandermans 2001, 320), that is, the belief that they have something in common. Notions of collective identity serve as a key socializing force in the development of social movements and even in individuals' will to fight back against oppression. Moreover, when women care about other women, or embrace feminist identities, they more often challenge sexist practices in society (Yoder, Tobias, and Snell 2011).

Claims of menstrual solidarity, then, may combat some of the toxicity surrounding menstruation, as women may use menstrual solidarity to fight back against sexism, sexist assumptions about menstruation, and menstrual shame. Speaking about menstruation at all can prove immensely difficult and provocative, as most women believe that the silence about their menstrual cycles is necessary (Kissling 1996a; Rose, Chrisler, and Couture 2008). Women who endorse menstrual synchrony, however, not only empower themselves personally but also break the silence by talking about menstruation (Bobel 2006). In short, menstrual solidarity moves menstruation out of the menstrual closet.

The Politics of Biology/The Biology of Politics

The literature on menstrual synchrony has several striking and unique features that speak to the discursive power of the phenomenon. First, researchers continue to study whether or not menstrual synchrony exists despite nearly forty years of conflict over the topic and substantial evidence that methodological errors may have biased results (Schank 2002). Second, the mainstream media have taken up menstrual synchrony as fact, a phenomenon not often seen in regard to the topic of women's bonds with other women (Rosewarne 2012). And, finally, despite (what we see as) fairly convincing evidence that menstrual synchrony does not consistently exist across populations (urban/rural, industrialized/nonindustrialized, heterosexual/lesbian), women themselves *want to believe in it.*

This desire to believe in menstrual synchrony may serve a variety of political purposes, as outlined earlier, which can, at least partially, explain why the scientific literatures remain hotly contested and why huge percentages of women nevertheless describe experiences with menstrual synchrony (Arden, Dye, and Walker 1999; Klebanoff and Keyser 1996). We theorize that declarations of menstrual synchrony do not result merely from "hearing a rumor" about its existence but, rather, that these claims have deep roots in women's *desires* to align themselves politically and personally with other women, particularly in light of sexist and patriarchal assumptions about menstruation. Assertions of menstrual solidarity have even appeared in poetry about menstruation, such as slam poet's Dominique Christina's (2014) claim, "When we're with our friends, our sisters, our mothers, our menstrual cycles will actually sync the fuck up . . . Everybody I love knows how to bleed with me. Hold on to that. There's a metaphor in it." Perhaps

Christina is correct; there *is* a metaphor in it, and this holds women not only to the belief in menstrual synchrony but to each other.

Women's assertions of, beliefs in, and perpetuation of menstrual solidarity raise several questions for future inquiry and interrogation: What do biological linkages and connections between women *achieve* politically, and why might they help the cause of social justice? Does the retrenchment of connections between women and their bodies (and women and nature) have a place in social movements to advance the cause of women's rights? Should social movements (and collective identities) rely on experiences of the body as a potential point of alignment between people, and, if so, how? Can science, popular culture, and political movements collide to produce, enhance, or erode women's solidarity with other women? And, finally, how must the project of solidarity take up areas typically dismissed as "too feminine," including connections between people and animals (Harris and Vitzthum 2013), solidarity produced by women-only spaces and experiences (Dunbar 1974), and (potentially erroneous) beliefs in menstrual synchrony?

Menstrual synchrony reveals the politics of biology; the seemingly scientific, empirical, neutral, bodily (and so on) occurrences measured by researchers of the body have far-reaching political implications. Connections between women based on biological and physiological experiences can create political alliances, foreground and background different scientific findings, and alter the relevance of science to our daily lives. Similarly, women's political connections to each other also have deeply biological roots, ones ripe for more exploration and assessment, deconstruction and celebration. In this moment where sex and gender are exploding into a multiplicity of categories, what does it mean to share something biological? Can (or should) the biological drive influence our political selves? And what is at stake in even asking such a question?

As a call for future research, we hope that scholars will take up such questions both theoretically and empirically. In-depth interviews with women about their beliefs in menstrual synchrony could prove especially interesting, as such data could help us to understand the conditions within which women validate the existence of menstrual synchrony. Ultimately, the debates about menstrual synchrony, and the persistent belief in its existence, point to the need for more spaces for women to feel in solidarity with each other, something that not only portrays a hopeful future for women but also paves the way for political and social progress.

2

The Menstrual Stain as Graffiti

Introduction

One of my psychotherapy patients—an adolescent girl prone to body image problems and boyfriend conflicts—has a recurring dream. In the dream, she is walking at school, starts her period without realizing it, and one of the kids at school points to the large menstrual stain on her pants and starts laughing. She looks down, notices that her white pants are dripping with blood, and hurries to the bathroom. But, she says, it is too late. Her menstrual blood has already stained every surface of her school—the chairs in the classrooms, the playground, the lunch room, other girls' clothes, even the bathroom mirror. She starts frantically washing things—her pants, the mirror, the ground—until she collapses in exhaustion and abruptly wakes up. This dream, she says, leaves her each time with feelings of terror.

Julia Kristeva, in her astute feminist analysis of the powers of horror, wrote of the abject body (i.e., the disgusting, gross, vile body) that it produces reactions in its audience by threatening a breakdown in meaning caused by loss of distinction between subject and object, self and other: "Abjection preserves what existed in the archaism of pre-objectal relationship, in the immemorial violence with which a body becomes separated from another body in order to be" (Kristeva 1982, 10). In other words, prior to when people can establish a clear separation between themselves and others, before people can understand their objects of desire, before they conceptualize the notion of representation, before they can clearly demarcate themselves from their opposites, before they can divide animals and humans or the primitive from the cultured, they had only the abject: shit, piss, vomit, decay, sweat, blood, pus, animality, murder, sex, leaks, and rupture.

According to Kristeva, all of these bodily fluids function to "erupt the Real" into our sanitized and body-denying lives, to force us to confront *not* the knowledge of death or the meaning of death (both far too symbolic and based in culture) but the "sort of materiality that traumatically *shows you* your own death" (4), that is, death itself, or, the inevitably dying body. Kristeva writes that seeing a human corpse, particularly that of a loved one, makes our own eventual death palpably real. With the decaying body present, we cannot escape the knowledge that our death *will exist* and that we cannot escape the inevitability of death. In short, the abject evokes "what disturbs identity, system, order. What does not respect borders, positions, rules" (4). Whatever sort of barrier placed between the knowledge of, or meaning around, death, and the *actual presence of death*, gets removed by the presence of the abject.

In light of Kristeva's claims about the abject, this essay interrogates the meaning of the menstrual stain in relation to the abject. That is, how does that browning, decaying, provocatively gendered symbol of "blood-turned-to-death" threaten to elicit these reactions by functioning not only as a *material symbol of death* but also as a highly gendered form of graffiti that attaches death to the *decaying, feminine, female body*? How does the process of "bleeding through," of using the menstrual stain to (unwittingly) leave a mark, provoke and disrupt boundaries, borders, and bodily order? Finally, what sorts of feminist resistances can be imagined in and through the menstrual stain as a transgressive representation of the abject?

Gendered Blood?

As scholars have astutely noted, blood gets infused with a variety of cultural interpretations, including violence, a symbol of passion or sexuality, the marker of life, and evidence of chaos (Lupton 1993; Seed 1985), but these representations most often work in relation to classic depictions of blood: blood as red, viscous, gooey, oozing, runny; blood that is, in short, *alive* within us. In this model, blood serves as an indicator of life, of "blood spilled" (as in war) or "blood shared" (as in family), but it remains, nearly always, a highly masculinized entity, infused with clear ideologies that *men* pass down their bloodlines, *men* battle each other in times of war, and *men* ultimately show power and sacrifice either through their own blood or by taking/eliciting another man's blood (McCracken 2003).

Menstrual blood, however, may have an oddly paradoxical association of death and life simultaneously intertwined. Perhaps the need to silence menstruating women, to ensure that they cannot reveal their actual menstrual blood as it comes out of them, relates to this threat of associating blood and power. The relative absence of thinking about or theorizing *gendered blood* (Lupton 1993) or of recognizing menstrual blood as powerful and female presents a significant gap in understanding the meanings of blood. Menstrual blood produces a narrative frankly opposite to most psychoanalytic and theoretical narratives about "femaleness." Rather than representing lack, want, absence, castration, masochism, and passivity, menstrual blood symbolizes *productivity*, presence, desire, threat, action, and perhaps even sadism. And yet, scholarly analyses of blood have largely neglected and failed to recognize menstrual blood as important and significant in its own right. Further still, psychoanalytic discourses have taken up (at length) analyzing other sites of bodily fluids and products (particularly semen, breast milk, feces) while menstrual blood remains largely undertheorized and underexamined (Ogden 1993; Yalom 1997).

How, then, can the *production* of fluid be theorized not in relation to the *alive* product of the body (gooey, dripping, clotty blood) but instead as the shadow or trace left behind by the (gendered) body? The menstrual stain, in contrast to menstrual blood itself, functions more in the classic sense of Kristeva's notion of the abject, as it signifies *not* the living, life-giving, pulsating, *alive* woman (as actual menstrual blood might do) but, rather, the decaying, dying, destructive, potentially fatal woman. This fusion of the abject-as-death narrative and the menstrual-blood-as-gendered-blood-of-power narrative creates in the viewer an absolute sense of panic. Not only does the menstrual stain disrupt the boundary between life and death (as all abject bodies do), but the menstrual stain also disrupts the boundary between women as lack/absence and women as powerful and even potentially violent. The menstrual stain *is* the *femme fatale*, a reminder of the death that women will meet but also, however irrationally perceived, the death that women will usher in and invite for men as well.

The bloody tampon, browning on the bathroom floor, leaking and bloated in the toilet bowl, shoved into the trash bin, and oozing into its toilet paper wrapping, pushes us to confront the border of our condition as living beings. To confront such an object *without* the referent of a bleeding woman—to see such horror divorced from the knowledge of its origin—brings, for men, a particularly profound sense of dread. They will die, and, perhaps, women will help that process along. This realization, encountered at the moment of seeing the bloody tampon, incites a surprised panic. As Kristeva wrote, "Abjection, on the other hand, is immoral, sinister, scheming, and shady: a terror that dissembles, a hatred that smiles, a passion that uses the body for barter instead of inflaming it, a debtor who sells you up, a friend who stabs you . . ." (4). The viewer must recoil in horror, separate him- or herself from this menstrual blood spatter, and force a separation in consciousness: "A massive and sudden emergence of uncanniness, which, familiar as it might have been in an opaque and forgotten life, now harries me as radically separate, loathsome. Not me. Not that. But not nothing, either" (Kristeva 1982, 2).

This twinning of browning menstrual blood and knowledge of (imminent) death may be partly responsible for why menstruation has so often been framed as *failed reproduction* (Martin 2001). Rather than seeing it as a cyclical part of life—as part of the cycles that bring life, give life, allow for the creation of breath—menstruation has been seen more as an ending, an unfertilization, a loss of something even while women's roles require reproduction for "successful womanhood." Girls learn that menstruation only carries within it the possibility of failure—failure to "properly" manage the blood, failure to "properly" conceal the blood, and failure to mimic the bodily processes of boys. As adults, women learn to see menstruation as inherently disappointing, frustrating, and difficult; in fact, most women describe menstruation using the language of dualism between the genders along with feelings of disgust and terror (Kissling 1996a; Lee 2002; Thornton 2013). Menstrual leaks, terrifying in their liminality between the genders, always subjected to patriarchal notions of containment and management, get framed throughout women's lives as something approaching misery and death (MacDonald 2007).

The phobic and panicky reaction to the menstrual stain—an even more extreme version of these deaths and failures—signifies this patriarchal construction of menstrual failure, menstrual loss, menstrual death. The menstrual stain, that imposition of women's bodies onto the "cultured" and "civilized" world, provokes a singular and peculiar horror in the onlooker. The stain *is itself a kind of death*, a preview of what is to come. As Kristeva noted,

> A wound with blood and pus, or the sickly, acrid smell of sweat, of decay, does not *signify* death. In the presence of signified death—a flat encephalograph, for instance—I would understand, react, or accept. No, as in true theater, without makeup or masks, refuse and corpses *show me* what I permanently thrust aside in order to live. . . . There, I am at the border of my condition as a living being. (1982, 3)

To discover a bloody tampon, to look down onto a chair stained with menstrual blood, is to inadvertently stumble (particularly for men) upon one's own actual, visceral, material death.

How, then, does a menstrual stain differ from other sorts of disembodied "products" of the body, particularly excrement? (And this question, however seemingly trivial, appears *constantly* in menstrual activism work, as some readers of *Re:Cycling* link together the exposure of menstrual blood or efforts to detach shame from menstruation with that of "celebrating feces" and such.) Kristeva differentiates excrement specifically as the danger to identity that comes from without: "the ego threatened by the non-ego, society threatened by its outside, life by death" (71), while menstrual blood stands for "the danger issuing from within the identity (social or sexual); it threatens the relationship between the sexes within a social aggregate and, through internaliza-tion, the identity of each sex in the face of sexual difference" (71). In other words, people become different through both sites (feces and menstrual blood), but because the boundaries between self/other are, in Kristeva's view, distinctly *female*—that is, we must powerfully differentiate and reject the mother in order to establish boundaries and order between the self and the other—menstrual blood more powerfully evokes this separation. The moment people *see* traces of menstrual blood, they are reminded, in essence, of the fundamental subconscious need to distance themselves from their own mothers and thereby establish the illusion that they will not actually die.

In short, Kristeva's position argues (critically) that the female body symbolizes pollution, "threatens one's *own and clean self*, which is the underpinning of any organization constituted by exclusions and hierarchies" (65). The unique and visceral hatred of, and disgust directed toward, menstrual blood functions as a way to maintain these hierarchies (women's bodies as "gross" and men's bodies as idealized) *in order to avoid facing death.* This highlights a particularly insidious aspect of the menstrual stain, for the fundamental ability to symbolically defy death (at least ideologically) comes from the rejection of the mother, the rejection of menstruating women (who symbolize mothers), and from the total annihilation of *any evidence that women menstruate at all* (and therefore symbolize menstruating, reproductive mothers). The menstrual stain must be obliterated, forgotten, washed away.

Menstrual blood, and especially traces of menstrual blood detached from the actual women who produced them, stands for the danger that comes from within the identity. The menstrual stain is the presence of women marked in graffiti onto the presence of men, a bloody mark made phallic, thrust into a public space. Without sexual difference and the suppression of all things woman, people cannot suppress an awareness of their imminent deaths; thus, the menstrual stain enters a context where it has been previously prohibited, and it disrupts this social contract, renders strange the boundaries between self and other, undoes the (sexist) binaries between bodies. The menstrual stain functions as a territorial marker, a signal of the impossibility of constraining and containing the female body and its troublesome fluids, and thus becomes a signal of the impossibility of diverting away from actual death. *It compulsively breaks down barriers.*

Bleeding through. Bleeding through. Bleeding through. Women use this phrase often, giving language to their menstrual blood that has crossed a barrier, pushed through a boundary, ruptured the existing social order. They have *bled through* not only their literal underwear and pants but also transformed the boundary between public/private, self/other, and animal/human. This boundary crossing, then, meets with the various resistances imposed by religion and art, two arenas that Kristeva theorizes as spaces for "purifying the abject." In other words, religion and art work to manage the terror of death, to stave off the panic that abject bodies produce. She writes, "The various means of *purifying* the abject—the various catharses—make up the history of religions, and end up with that catharsis par excellence called art, both on the far and near side of religion" (17). The boundary crossing itself—the production of the menstrual stain—cannot attach to language, art, or religion, and will be necessarily thrown away, discarded, erased, and eradicated.

Only in language can we begin to reconnect death with life, rejoin in language the stain with the alive menstruating body, and transform the meaning of the abject. Still, Kristeva would say that this is just language, a "language of want, of the fear that edges up to it and runs along its edges" (38). Writing about abjection creates space for the hope that such catharsis will protect us from horror itself, but such writing is merely "an impure process that protects from the abject only by dint of being immersed in it" (29). In this regard, Kristeva ultimately suggests that theorizing about something as abject as menstrual blood and menstrual stains can only lead to terror itself; short of uprooting patriarchal (and psychoanalytic) claims about women's bodily fluids as an inherent signifier of horror and death, we are left only with partial language, traces, shadows, hauntings, slight possibilities, hints, and suggestions at the margin.

Part Two

Dispatches from the Blogosphere

3

In Praise of Cycles

As a professor and therapist, I see many people come through the door who struggle with a variety of feelings they identify as problematic to their lives: depression, anxiety, mania, suicidal thoughts, panic, grief, boredom, anger (and so on). We are taught, as therapists, to see the cycles of mood as an inherent problem—something indicative of a "mood disorder," something to keep on high alert about, to monitor, to control, to consider medicating (Hinshaw 2007). Men, in particular, learn to internalize the idea that they must avoid emotional cycles, sadness, and anything associated with "weakness" and so-called "femininity." While I do not deny the existence of some cyclic mood disorders—where people experience episodes of severe negative feelings, bipolar feelings, or intense anxieties that causes notable distress—it does seem problematic, both within and outside of therapy, that people so often consider cycles detrimental.

Never is this disdain of cycles more evident than in people's descriptions of women's menstrual cycles as inherently troubling (Roberts 2004). Women often report negative side effects of menstruation, particularly feeling moodier, less energetic, more bloated, angrier, less sexual, hungrier, and more vulnerable (and many men, too often, quickly hurl these cyclic changes into women's faces as an insult). Women say these fluctuations bother them because they like to feel "normal" (that is, emulating men who supposedly lack emotional and physical cycles). But, isn't the fundamental nature of things quite . . . cyclic?

Nearly everything that comes in cycles has potential benefits, teaching us that the world is fluid, ever-changing, always in flux. The changing seasons (even in Phoenix where I live, where the seasons move from pleasantly warm to unbearably hot) signal the onset of

new weather patterns, shorter or longer days, and necessary undula-
tions and differences. Growing up in the West, I have heard people
who have roots in the East Coast and the Midwest lament the loss
of changing seasons when they move to California or Arizona—they
want the rhythms, pace, sensory experiences, and visual scenery that
accompanies the traditional four seasons existence.

We are creatures that crave cycles. Academics rely on the ebbs
and flows of the academic year to guide their work, pausing in the
summer and over the holiday break for some much-needed rest before
starting again each school year with full gusto. College professors'
job satisfaction is among the highest of all professions (CNN Money
2012a; Mottax 1985), alongside computer programmers, who overwhelmingly set their own hours, and engineers and physical therapists,
who have more autonomy than most American workers. (Cross-
culturally, European workers generally report more happiness as well,
as Europe generally recognizes the cyclic nature of life by offering
extended vacation time, paid maternity leave, and generous sick pay.)
More and more American companies have started giving employees
periodic sabbaticals (CNN Money 2012b), acknowledging that larger
chunks of time to shift focus, relax, start a new project, or travel will
earn company loyalty and will markedly increase job satisfaction. The
monotony of the year-round, nine-to-five job with little vacation time
and, more importantly, no cycles of work and play creates the most
havoc on people's lives. Shift workers who disrupt the natural cycles
of their bodies—staying up all night, sleeping all day—have poor life
expectancies (Griffin 2012), substantially higher risks for at least six
different kinds of cancer (Huffington Post 2012), more heart attacks,
and far poorer health outcomes as a result (Knutsson 2003). Even
those who take antidepressants and antianxiety medication—perhaps
to lift them out of their low moods or panicky states—often report
feeling apathetic and robotic as a side effect (Price, Cole, and Goodwin
2009), missing, it seems, the cycles of mood they once had.

The disdain for cycles, the need to convince people that they
should never feel too sad nor too happy (Fischer et al. 2004), the
loathing we seem to direct toward the menstruating body (Johnston-
Robledo et al. 2003), and the insistence that people work themselves
to death without breaks or cyclic expenditures of energy all result
from the dangerous fusion of patriarchy, capitalism, and the pharmaceutical industry (Sennett 2011). The dogged insistence that people

must always be happy, must work until they drop without ever taking time to fully rest, must always "manage" the cycles of their bodies (for example, losing their baby weight right after pregnancy, controlling menstrual blood, forcing themselves to work following a death in the family, clocking in the same hours year round, bragging about overexertions while sick), reveals a deep-seated disavowal of cycles as fundamental to human life. Cycles matter—they reflect the truths women have always known, the necessity of change and movement, the power of the body to teach us about the world and, perhaps, to undermine the institutions that deplete and eradicate the natural cycles of human life in favor of sexism and profit. As a single example, one study found that women felt more menstrual joy when they read material about the health benefits of menstrual cycles (Chrisler et al. 1994), implying that reframing our thinking about cycles matters to our well-being. The denial of cycles also underlies some of the core processes behind social alienation (Roscigno and Hodson 2004) and body objectification (Schooler et al. 2005), implying that, by embracing cycles, we may also improve other aspects of our lives.

What would it mean instead to embrace cycles, to praise and celebrate them, and to recognize the ways in which we already do so in many of our most cherished rituals? If we take the energy we already expend celebrating cyclic and seasonal aspects of our lives—winter holidays, summer vacations, rituals of harvest and fall weather, spring bloom, full moons, and so on—and apply these to our own moods, bodies, and rhythms, we may find a wealth of surprising opportunities for self-affirmation and even collective recognition of the importance of cycles. These changes are the fundamental building blocks of ritual, pleasure, joy, and even life and death; attending to them connects us more fully to the process of being alive.

4

"Feminine Hygiene" and the Ultimate Double Standard

Most women have had the unfortunate experience of realizing that they have started their periods at an inconvenient time or place, without proper backup, having to rely on clunky and sporadically available tampon dispensers in public restrooms. When driving across the country recently, I stopped near Albuquerque at a small gas station and entered the unisex restroom frantically searching for a tampon machine. Instead, I found a large, brightly colored condom machine fastened prominently on the wall that featured four options: "ribbed for her pleasure" condoms, extra-large condoms, packages of lube, and a "grab bag" of "sexual surprises." A nearby wall above the toilet seat featured a prominent sign: *DO NOT FLUSH FEMININE HYGIENE PRODUCTS DOWN THE TOILET OR IT WILL CLOG OUR SYS-TEM.* Feeling unusually irked by this duality—the cheery availability of (men's) safer sex products and the utter disdain for women's menstrual products—I contemplated the bigger problem of this gendered bathroom dilemma: Women's bodies—leaky and troublesome—are too often constructed with the context of disease, inconveniences, contamination, and *un*hygienic fixations (Case and Lippard 2009). Men, on the other hand, receive props for their "leakages" (e.g., urine, farts, semen) as humorous, fun, playful, and sometimes even sexy; in some cases, semen is even seen as heroic, glorified, and highly valued (Moore 2008). (I recently realized how rarely menstruation is treated with humor or fun when I felt an uncommon joy at bleeding into my black-and-blue skull-and-crossbones patterned reusable Lunapads.)

47

I loathe the term *feminine hygiene* for a host of reasons. At its most benign, the term gives vague descriptors for what women use to manage their menstrual cycles, giving additional cultural momentum behind the general refusal to deal with nuance and specifics of a menstruating vagina (or vaginas at all, frankly). When stores, advertisements, and signs evoke *feminine hygiene*, they suggest, linguistically, that the words *tampon, pad,* or *cup* seem scary. The phrase *feminine hygiene* implies "products to keep the unkempt, unruly, unhygienic, dirty, unsanitary, bloody vagina in check" rather than simply stating the actual terms for what women use. (It also needlessly genders the already-gendered process of menstruation.) Men's products, for example, do not use such euphemisms and instead directly refer to their function (e.g., razor, deodorant, aftershave). Why not use a less pejorative and more descriptive phrase like *menstrual products*?

The bizarre throwback to the 1950s represented by the continued use of *feminine hygiene* has serious trickle-down effects on people's attitudes about menstruation. First, as Elizabeth Kissling (2006) showed, people still feel palpable anxiety about purchasing menstrual products in the store or discussing menstruation openly, in part because the marketing and packaging of menstrual products have a long history of playing on women's anxieties about their bodies (Erchull et al. 2002). Many people do not even know the terms *menstrual* or *menstruation* as commonly understood words (White 2013). I blame *feminine hygiene* for this.

Second, by framing menstrual products as products devoted to cleanliness and management of otherwise "vile" bodily fluids, *feminine hygiene* products get spatially placed near products of excrement like diapers and incontinence merchandise in the store. A typical sign will read: "Feminine Hygiene, Diapers, Personal Care" in these aisles of the grocery store. Years ago, a student of mine visited over twenty-five grocery stores and pharmacies and found that nearly every single store placed tampons and pads directly beside diapers (not only linking menstruation to defecation but also implying that adult women's products should coexist with children's products). The use of *hygiene* here links menstrual blood with feces, urine, and products that infantilize women and their bodies. It also implicitly links the *feminine* (another bizarre word that is rarely attached commercially to anything besides menstrual products) with women needing to clean their own *and* others' messy bodies.

My third concern about *feminine hygiene* is that we don't fully understand the history of the (d)evolving phrase. As Andrea Tone (1996) found, *feminine hygiene* originally referred to birth control rather than menstrual products. A 1933 advertisement in *McCall's* for Lysol's feminine hygiene products read:

> The most frequent eternal triangle:
>
> A HUSBAND . . . A WIFE . . . and her FEARS
>
> Fewer marriages would flounder around in a maze of
> misunderstanding and unhappiness if more wives knew
> and practiced regular marriage hygiene. Without it,
> some minor physical irregularity plants in a woman's
> mind the fear of a major crisis. Let so devastating a fear
> recur again and again, and the most gracious wife turns
> into a nerve-ridden, irritable travesty of herself.

Translation: Use feminine hygiene (birth control) if men want to avoid their wives turning down sex because they're scared of pregnancy. Over the next twenty years, the phrase later transitioned from a reference to birth control into a reference for female douches (an ad touted: "There are some things a husband just can't mention to his wife!") and finally into a phrase about managing menstruation. Why this particular version of the *feminine hygiene* phrase has stuck with us so forcefully, and why we insist on vague and unspecific terminology for menstrual products, relates directly to broader discourses of panic around, and ignorance about, women's reproduction, menstruation, and vaginal health. What would a product designed for *masculine hygiene* look like, and what would it clean up? These linguistic choices, while seemingly benign, hold immense implications for powerful (and less powerful) bodies and identities. While not a perfect solution— as tampons and pads themselves are largely wasteful and not always good for women's health—doing away with outdated and frankly antifeminist phrases like *feminine hygiene* signals a step toward better acknowledging the continued impact of these sexist historical relics.

5

Adventures on Komodo Island

During my more rugged travel experiences, I have often found myself confronted with the formidable task of facing the limitations and boundaries of my physical self. While in India, for example, I often had to contemplate the dilemma of drinking water (and therefore needing to urinate in places where clean restrooms did not exist) or becoming dehydrated. (This problem kills malnourished children in developing countries while it merely poses an embarrassing inconvenience for those with generally good health.) On another trip, I had become ill from food and/or water poisoning and had vomited violently for two days, leaving my body empty of calories and unable to climb up a sizeable hill to see a grand historical fort. Halfway up that hill, my normally spunky and determined self had a revelation about my newly reimagined ideas about the relationship between food and energy. Travel sometimes pushes us to the edge of our capacity for exertion, and it certainly provokes new understandings of body norms.

On a trip to Indonesia, I had the opportunity to visit Komodo Island, home of the infamous Komodo dragons. Before I left, my then six-year-old nephew informed me (gleefully) that these creatures are extremely dangerous and kill people and animals by biting them, allowing multitudes of mouth bacteria to infect the body, and watching them slowly die (Bull, Jessop, and Whiteley 2010). The dragons can then follow around the dying animal and consume their corpses once their prey is left defenseless and paralyzed with bacterial infection. Before arriving on the island, our guide told our group similar stories about the dangers of the Komodo dragon: There is no antivenin equivalent for Komodo dragons, and, as such, people die every year by accidentally trekking alone or mistaking Komodo for another Indonesian island. Unsuspecting tourists die often enough that park rangers must now escort guests on the island as a mandatory safety measure. Precautions of every sort must be taken.

Just prior to our arrival, excited for the chance to see Komodo dragons in their natural habitat, I received a notice in my room saying that menstruating women could not step foot on the island of Komodo and that only nonmenstruating women could enter the island. The notice also informed visitors that people with wounds could not visit the island (though it did not specify the type and size of wound it was referring to), and visitors could not wear backpacks or clothing with any red on them. Komodo dragons have a particular combination of aggression, keen smell, bad eyesight, and bloodlust (Ciofi 1999; Vidal 2008). I later learned that gender segregation also applies to the locals on Komodo, as women cannot work in jobs near the dragon's habitats and, consequently, are largely segregated from men and kept indoors (Walpole and Goodwin 2000).

As a critical feminist, I initially refused to believe the reality of the caution against menstruating women, imagining that it must be yet another method of excluding women from "men's" activities like trekking, hiking, and exploring the island. Did these cautions simply represent a repackaging of the menstrual hut idea? Would menstruating women actually inspire attacks? Did menstrual blood have a particular scent that differentiated it from other kinds of blood? What about women who lived on Komodo Island? How could resident Komodo women protect themselves? Was the ban yet another sexist maneuver to control women and their bodies? Inquiring about this menstrual ban, I learned that the dragons can smell blood for up to five miles and, lacking the ability to discern their dying prey from menstruating women, could mistake menstruating women for dying animals and kill them. A series of attacks on menstruating women have been documented on the island, leading the rangers to warn menstruating women that they must not come near Komodo dragons under any circumstance (Schiff 2010).

My next thoughts focused on the actual disclosure of women's menstrual status. Typically, questions about menstruation in the United States are often considered prying and impolite; few strangers in the United States and other Asian countries feel entitled to directly ask women about their menstrual status (Koutroulis 2001; Mutunda 2006). Would the park rangers actually *ask* women about their menstrual status? Could a menstruating woman who lied about, or refused to disclose, her status put the group at risk? When I started inquiring about this further, I found that discussions about Komodo Island presented one of the only contexts I have ever encountered when menstrual status could be discussed across genders, ages, races, and cultures, as the notice of warning inspired the group I was traveling with to discuss menstruation openly in ways I had never personally witnessed before. Over dinner the night before our arrival in Komodo, the group discussed menstruation critically, frankly, and in unusual detail. Even though the discourse included (somewhat traditional) notions of "protecting women," it also provoked the group to consider some of the questions I had asked about the cultural and gendered aspects of menstrual disclosure. Getting comfortable with the topic was not an option for the menstruating women in the group, as they had to openly disclose their status regardless of whether they would prefer to keep it secret. Never before had any of us confronted the idea of security personnel who would confirm whether we were currently menstruating (a subject that provoked more serious consideration of TSA intrusions on people's personal lives as well) (Kissling 2010).

Once on the island, walking among the trees and through the dusty landscape behind our ranger who carried only a large stick with a forked end, my childlike glee at the Indiana Jones–like qualities of the adventure superseded my fear of Komodo dragon attack. When we finally found the dragons, lazing about in clusters near a spot in the late afternoon shade, I felt a twinge of gratitude that my body had decided not to bleed that day. In my normal life, battling the stereotypes and secrecy that surround menstruation, confronting the shame and silence women face about their menstrual cycles, this new-found idea of menstruation as a kind of animal communication felt like a welcome diversion. Menstruation as *danger*, as physical *threat*, as something that could put oneself or one's travel mates *in jeopardy* seemed unusually exotic, bizarre, and surreal. (That said, it also signaled typically patriarchal ideas of men protecting women from dangerous things, see Moya et al. 2007.) Even more interestingly, the ability to discuss menstruation so openly with such a unique mix of people, under such strange circumstances, provided the opportunity to attach menstrual status to adventure and to remind myself that the narratives Americans have about menstruation—typically filled with secrecy, shame, and silence—do not yet pervade every corner of the globe.

6

Menstruation according to Apple

The repetition of all things pink connected to all things related to women's health has started to seem omnipresent. First, the pharmaceutical companies released pink containers for birth control pills, followed by the pink repackaging of Prozac (renamed Sarafem) to treat premenstrual dysphoric disorder (PMDD) (Kissling 2006). Then came the reductive and ferociously popular pink ads, logos, banners, and yogurt containers of the Susan G. Komen Breast Cancer Foundation (Bodkin 2012). (Pro football players even wore pink shoes to distance themselves from the stereotype of the "wife beater," see King 2006.) Next came special dye that restored women's so-called natural pink color to their labia ("My New Pink Button"), reminding women (especially women of color) that their brown and gray and flesh-colored labia were not . . . pink enough? It's not surprising, then, that the most popular menstruation apps for the iPhone and iPad—Period Tracker, iPeriod, Period Diary, and Monthly Cycle—have a similar pink, flowery, and decidedly "girlie" vibe. Anything designed for women's bodies apparently has to infantilize women by looking like Strawberry Shortcake and Barbie, even well into women's adult lives. But complaints about these apps do not end at mere aesthetics.

The app Period Tracker creates a particular brand around what it means to menstruate, reinforcing stereotypical goals for women to marry, reproduce, and maintain traditional gendered scripts (Gillespie 2003). Much like the messages featured in advertisements for pregnancy tests—which emphasize women's longing for pregnancy and their unadulterated joy at finding out the news of their pregnancy—Period Tracker also frames the purpose of the app as a fertility-monitoring tool, even though reviews of the app suggest that most women use it to do what the title says: to track periods. The assumptions that women want to become pregnant extend into many features of the app: when a woman ovulates, flowers appear on the otherwise-barren tree, reminding her to seek out a sperm provider; during menstruation, the app starts a countdown, allowing women to tick off the number of days they have endured their cycle; green dots appear for the days women can get pregnant; and, finally, the app features a tool where women can track "intimacy." (Apparently, the word *sex* is too gauche for the world of period-tracker apps, leaving *intimacy* as a code for sexual intercourse.)

Further, Period Tracker has a variety of built-in ways to attach menstruation—and the menstrual cycle in general—to shame and negativity. The app allows women to track a variety of symptoms throughout their cycle, but every single one of these has negative connotations of pain and misery, playing into women's fears of "properly" managing their menstrual symptoms (Santer, Wyke, and Warner 2008). Acne. Backaches. Bloating. Body Aches. Constipation. Cramps. Cravings (Salty). Cravings (Sweet). Dizziness. Spotting. Headaches. Indigestion. Insomnia. Joint Pains. Nausea. Neck Aches. Tender Breasts. In the list of moods one can track, the first two listed are *angry* and *anxious*. Joy, happiness, relaxed, and other positive emotions do not appear at all. Period Tracker also alerts women to the start date of their period, but it does so by referring to it as, simply, "P," implying that if someone saw a period start–date alert that appeared using the language of "periods" on a woman's phone, it would shame the owner of the phone.

Other period apps also have a variety of similar features, emphasizing the "girlie" qualities of menstrual cycles and the all-important goal of pregnancy. The app iPeriod has specific code words for sex, as it calls sex a "love connection," allows three options for mood— normal, sad, and irritable—and constructs pregnancy as the ultimate goal of tracking the menstrual cycle. PeriodPlus, a newer app with over a million users, features a pink color scheme and a purple bunny that dispenses weird pieces of self-help wisdom alongside cute "girlie" graphics, while the app Glow invites users to do things like call their best friend to de-stress from the monstrous menstrual period or relax and do yoga to calm their raging hormones (Hines 2013).

All of this emphasis on pregnancy, menstrual negativity, and the "monstrous" symptoms of PMS and menstruation obscures the fundamentally important (and feminist!) work of tracking one's menstrual cycle for positive and decidedly non-fertility-related reasons: Most obviously, to anticipate our period's starting date, but less obviously, to understand and track the body's rhythms, to actively avoid pregnancy, to know ourselves more deeply, to appreciate our cycles, to better predict menstruation and how it coordinates with our schedules, to accurately assess whether we have experienced a drastic change in our normal rhythms, to track a female partner's cycles, to signal the start of menopause or irregular cycling, to keep an eye on heavy periods versus light periods, and to feel more in tune with our bodies (among others).

Why can't a period tracker allow women to celebrate the menstrual cycle or see the arrival of menstruation as joyous or positive? Why can't apps track positive bodily changes like "Increased Libido," "Elevated Mood," and "Heightened Sensitivity"? I want a period tracker that dumps the hot-pink color, the swirling flowers that only bloom during ovulation, the adamantly pro-pregnancy angle, the sex-phobic language, the heterosexism, and the shaming of women's menstrual cycles in favor of a radically reimagined, positive, celebratory mode of menstrual charting. Knowing more about our cycles has long roots in our feminist history—technology should reflect the diversity of the menstrual experience.

7

Collateral Damage

Throwing Menstruation Out of the Museum

The media has recently focused much attention on the Smithsonian Museum's decision to pull the David Wojnarowicz video "A Fire in My Belly" from an exhibition at the National Portrait Gallery in Washington, D.C., titled, *Hide/Seek* (Itzkoff 2010). Part of "the first major museum exhibition to focus on sexual difference in the making of modern American portraiture," the piece depicted the suffering of an HIV-positive man along with ants crawling on a crucifix. The museum apologized for the piece's contents after a group of Republican representatives and the Catholic League demanded the removal of the video. U.S. representative Jack Kingston of Georgia called it "in your face perversion paid for by tax dollars" (Dobrzynski).

This scenario is far from unique, as the issue of censoring sex (alongside feminism and female artists in general) in museums has a long and contentious history both in the United States and abroad (Wagner 2010). For much of the 1950s through the 1980s museums excluded sex in its entirety from the story of human existence, deeming it offensive and obscene (Frost 2008). Recent decades have seen some progress in this regard, but clear omissions still exist. For example, prostitution is rarely featured in museums despite public interest in various "scandals" associated with sex work (Adams and Frances 2003). In the late 1980s, the National Endowment for the Arts (NEA) engaged in fierce battles about whether to fund so-called obscene shows, often equating obscenity with explicitly gay and lesbian content (e.g., Robert Mapplethorpe's photography). Museums like the Chicago Art Institute and the Metropolitan Museum of Art in New York City have battled over the morality and ethics of censoring sex in the museum (Semonche 2007). Greek vases and objects depicting explicit sexual acts have been deemed unfit for children's viewing and have been removed from major museums throughout the world. The National Museum of Erotica in Canberra, Australia, shut down over controversies surrounding its explicit portrayal of sexual artifacts (Lalor and Gorman 2012).

So how might this relate to the menstruating body? I recently visited one of my favorite museums in the world—the Heard Museum of American Indian Art and History in Phoenix, Arizona. They had several anthropological exhibits revolving around family life, ritual, and celebrations of coming-of-age among indigenous cultures in the Southwest. One exhibit featured paintings of ceremonies practiced among Native American communities of the Southwest. Another exhibit on Apache life featured several cases of clothing with text dedicated to women's initiation into womanhood following the onset of puberty. Notably, the word *menstruation* and any depiction of women's menstrual blood were entirely absent from both of these exhibits. This presents an especially puzzling omission because Apache communities believe that girls become women immediately after menarche (Farrer 1980). Discussions of preparation of food, flowers, and clothing by elderly members of the girls' communities were featured prominently, along with the significance of women learning how to transition to womanhood. Almost certainly, this ritualized process revolved around the onset of women's menstrual cycles, yet no mention of women's menarche occurred.

I wondered: Has the menstruating body suffered from the collateral damage of censoring sex? Do we associate all aspects of the (leaky, disgusting, abject) female body with the "sinful" and "harmful-to-children" rhetoric of sexually explicit museum materials? When men's "powerful" ejaculations (Jackson Pollock!) and phallic powers are celebrated symbolically, why do women's cycling bodies hold such a taboo place in museum culture? What would it mean if menstruation held a more prominent place in museums in general?

Taboos surrounding the entrance of menstruation into museums continue in full force. Though a few radical feminist performance artists have featured work on menstruation (for example, Linder Sterling's menstrual jewelry, or Mako Idemitsu's 1973 piece "What a Woman Made," featuring photos of bloody tampons), the normally edgy, provocative, and forward-thinking art world has yet to fully recognize menstruation as a valid subject of interest. The backlash against the Museum of Menstruation and Women's Health (MUM), once located in Carrollton, Maryland, and now featured only online, reveals just how much difficulty the public has accepting menstruation as a valid subject of analysis. In a 2007 article discussing the "10 Most Bizarre Museums," MUM is listed alongside the Toilet Museum, the Voodoo Museum, the Museum of the Penis, and the Burger Museum. In another article on "The 7 Most Horrifying Museums on Earth," MUM takes company with museums on child mummies, psychiatric patients, ventriloquism, fetuses in jars, and ancient phalluses (Quercia 2010). Harry Finley, the founder and curator of MUM, said in a 2010 interview:

> [Menstruation] is not a polite thing to talk about in casual society. I've gotten so used to this now that it's no big deal for me. But it is for other people. Especially coming from some guy. I really get, sometimes, a horrified reaction. I can tell by the stares and the silence. Even from liberal people. When I started the museum, I thought, "Oh boy, this would not bother them." But it still bothers basically everybody. Almost every reaction is negative. . . . I think a lot of it is the association of a male doing this. Like, what is his interest in this? (Hess 2010)

The assumptions of deviance for a man interested in the history and cultural silences surrounding menstruation, or the assumption that menstruation cannot have an explicit place in the coming-of-age stories depicted in an exhibition explicitly about coming-of-age, both reveal just how far we have to travel with regard to menstrual acceptance, activism, and awareness. Somehow, the link between the "taboo" body and the "obscene" aspects of sexuality has grown stronger, almost invisibly, in the kinds of stories we tell about ourselves. This absence represents yet another calculated denial of the cycling body, of bodies that leak and shift and leave stains. I yearn to see depictions of the menstruating body featured prominently in the story of women, culture, and society. The censoring of these experiences, however unintentional, reduces and redefines women's experiences of their bodies in ways that further alienate them from the power and cultural significance of menstruation.

Part Three

Blood on the Couch

8

Blood on the Couch

Disclosures about Menstruation in the Therapy Room

Introduction

As a feminist therapist who has maintained a private practice for many years, it never fails to surprise me how often, and in what ways, patients bring up the topic of menstruation during sessions. In my professor role, I *study* menstruation, after all, so I may be primed to remember when women mention their menstrual cycles, but it does seem striking that so little scholarship has examined the therapeutic implications and processing around a topic that arises with great regularity during therapy sessions. This essay explores disclosures about menstruation from three different former women patients of mine in order to explore how menstruation functions in the private space of therapist-patient exchange. Specifically, by unpacking the ways that menstruation works as a (unmentionable) taboo, a mode of alliance with the therapist, an expression of personal distress, and a way to assert assumptions about other women's cycles and experiences, menstruation in therapy presents a compelling opportunity to interrogate gender and power and to examine the diffuse boundaries between the public and private. Women often feel quite ambivalent about their menstrual cycles; such ambivalence opens up spaces for productive conversations about its meaning (Marván, Morales, and Cortés-Iniestra 2006; Santer, Wyke, and Warner 2008). Ultimately, I argue in this essay that women experience strongly paradoxical feelings about their menstrual cycles, seeing them on the one hand as a source of intense personal distress and, on the other, as a site of resistance, emotional expression, and way of feeling reproductively "normal."

Because my practice specializes in issues of sexuality, gender, and trauma, I have treated many women throughout the years in my therapy practice, the majority of whom organically disclose their menstrual cycle status to me at some point over the course of therapy. In some ways, these disclosures are surprising, as research shows that over two-thirds of clinical patients routinely withhold important facts from their therapists, most often related to sexual and body shame (Farber 2003). Their interpreted meanings behind menstruation, and the way they discuss it, reflects important tensions about the fusion between the public and private, and the personal/intimate aspects of menstruation as it relates to metanarratives about menstruation. Similar to Elizabeth Kissling's (1996b) findings that girls learn to separate the "scientific" from the "practical" aspects of menstruation, women in therapy often describe their menstrual status using language of affinity, practicality, and emotionality.

The following case studies describe different aspects of menstruation that women discussed in therapy with me; I chose these three cases as examples of the wide emotional range that women can experience around menstruation. (Note that, with the approval of the Institutional Review Board from Arizona State University, I collected case study data from several patients over the course of five years. Each of these patients consented to have their case material included in published studies, and all participants were assigned a pseudonym to protect their identities.) Though quite different in their personal backgrounds, reasons for seeking psychotherapy, openness to discussing their problems, and quality of dialogue, these cases present a fuller picture of menstrual discourse and its relevance to psychotherapy work.

Rosie

Rosie, a thirty-nine-year-old married Latina woman with three children, entered therapy initially seeking help for problems with her family and difficulties with feeling motivated to get out of bed in the morning. During her initial visit, she described her family background as strict and strongly religious, noting that her father had required absolute obedience in order to return love and affection. Having grown up in a large family, she recalled that she and her siblings would be called to dinner with a whistle, that they had numerous household chores, and that their mother remained silent and passive for most of their childhood together. Rosie identified herself as a feminist who had "broken free" of her past by marrying a savvy, fun, and well-off government official. The two had married at age twenty, raised a family of three children, and had worked hard to maintain a good marriage. That said, his marital infidelity with a family friend left Rosie feeling in despair about the future of her marriage. The two had not slept in the same bed together for some time, and she reported that she had given up on him but did not want to formally divorce him because she wanted to protect the happiness of her teenage children.

During our third session, Rosie brought up her menstrual cycle for the first time, saying that she "didn't usually talk about this," but that she wanted to let me know that she struggled with her mood more often during her period. When I inquired more about this, she described her childhood stories of menstruation as the ultimate taboo. Her mother, squeamish about all things related to her daughters' bodies and sexualities, had never talked about menstruation, and her father, a strict military man intent on raising "good sons" (even with his female children) refused to acknowledge Rosie's menstrual cycles. (Indeed, several studies have referenced the difficulty of talking about menstruation with one's parents, particularly a father, see Koff and Reirdan 1995.) As an adolescent, Rosie had started her period by feeling fear and distress and thinking that she was dying, only to find out from a school friend that what she had experienced was quite normal. Still, when she told her mother about starting her period, her mother refused to buy any pads or tampons and told her to "deal with it yourself."

This history of menstrual shame, denial, and suppression appeared in full force for Rosie as an adult. During one session, she talked about how, during her period, she felt disgusting and gross, noting that she took showers obsessively and tried hard to clean herself often and with vigor. "You know what I mean," she said, "It's *just awful. It's something I wish I didn't have to experience anymore at all.*" For Rosie, the menstrual taboo had also translated into difficulty talking to her newly menstruating daughter about periods. Though she had (reluctantly and shamefully) bought her daughter some pads and showed her how to use them, she feared telling her husband about her daughter's period. Further, Rosie never mentioned her menstrual cycle to her husband. When I asked how they discussed it, she said, "I just tell him that I had a visitor today" followed by a series of physical complaints. (This also fits with a recent study that found that people talk about menstruation on Twitter as something filled with irrationality, moodiness, neediness, suffering, cruelty, and anger; see Thornton 2013.)

Despite Rosie's clear avoidance of using direct language about menstruation with her husband, she willingly discussed her own periods during our therapy time, a contradiction that revealed a striking parallel to some of her other presenting problems. For Rosie, therapy served as a space to unleash her feelings that she had kept pent up, particularly as she described her anger at her father, her disappointment in her mother, and her ambivalence about her failing marriage and the betrayals she experienced with her husband. In therapy, she said, she could talk about anything and no one would know. Rosie made a point to reveal her "menstrual status" on several occasions to me (that is, whether she was premenstrual or currently on her period), something I framed as a rebellion against her strict upbringing. Intent on other kinds of bodily rebellion, Rosie had also recently bought her first vibrator and had discussed (in rather vague language) her experimentation with masturbation.

Still, Rosie struggled to embrace her body and feel desirable. As someone who had grown up working class and who had befriended mostly lesbians and men during her teenage years, she hated anything she considered too feminine and had in some ways adopted her father's mentality about good femininity. (Her father, of course, never treated her mother as a "good woman" and had always ridiculed her mother as rather stupid and boring.) For Rosie, embracing her body, trying to find a comfortable femininity, and becoming increasingly self-reliant had proven difficult challenges to tackle at once. Working through her feelings about her menstrual cycle had, for Rosie, resulted in growing confidence about her ability to self-define and rebel against the restrictive norms of her youth.

Ultimately, menstruation functioned as a centerpiece for the therapy work about Rosie's presenting problems. By talking frankly about menstruation both concretely and as a symbol for other aspects of Rosie's life, we could address seemingly unrelated issues that funneled into menstrual conversations. Specifically, menstruation allowed open discourse about her history with her parents, her resentment about not expressing herself in her marriage, her budding feminist ideas and gendered rebellions, and her goals to feel more confident about her body and her sexuality.

Linda

Linda, a forty-five-year-old single, white "wild child," began a year-long course of therapy in which she sought help for emotional mood swings, difficulty in her current romantic relationships, and problems related to childhood sexual abuse. A passionate and difficult patient, Linda had a tendency to speak loudly in therapy, to send angry and abusive text messages to people she felt agitated with, and to fluctuate between idealization and rejection of people in her life (including, at times, me as her therapist). Linda described her history as full of conflict and strife; since her mother had died when she was in her twenties, she rarely spoke to her father, and she was estranged from her three siblings, all of whom lived out of state. A mother of two children, she frequently encountered difficulties managing money and coping with the stresses of parenting alongside her responsibilities at work and in her romantic relationship.

Joan Chrisler (2008) once theorized that the menstrual cycle presented women with a socially acceptable reason to express anger and rage and that "premenstrual syndrome" served as code for socially acceptable anger. As Chrisler said, "Women are supposed to be cheerleaders. . . . When a woman is anything but that, she and her family are quick to think something is wrong. . . . The discourse is me, not me, my real self, my PMS self. It allows you to hold onto a view of yourself as a good mother who doesn't lose her temper" (quoted in Daw 2002, 58). For Linda, her menstrual cycles gave her permission to feel what she felt for most of the month but did not express: extreme anger. During her premenstrual time and during her periods, Linda went into fits of rage at her boyfriend, angry that he did not value her enough, that he looked at other women, that he did not call or text when he said he would, that he would not commit to marrying her. Linda felt she *could* be angry only while menstruating. Once, during an altercation in which she pushed her boyfriend and screamed at him in a restaurant, Linda ended up in jail overnight for disorderly conduct. During our session the following week, Linda disclosed that she believed this behavior stemmed from her period and that her menstrual cycle had "made her crazy."

In her well-known work on the links between women and madness, Phyllis Chesler (2005) argued that depression represents anger turned inward toward the self, as most women had no outlet for their rage. Chesler argued that our culture labels women as crazy when they perform as passive but also when they express anger or show too much emotion. "Women are seen as sick when they act out the female role (are depressed, incompetent, frigid, anxious) *and* when they reject the female role (are hostile, successful, sexually active)—especially with other women" (Chesler 2005, 56). This story of excess, of "too muchness," had followed Linda around for much of her life. In trouble for spending too much money, having too much sex, and being perpetually drawn toward chaos, she had been a hell-raiser for most of her youth and during her twenties. After a brief marriage to an abusive husband, she divorced and ran through her 401k and the divorce settlement in a matter of months. "I get crazy when I'm PMS-ing," she told me. "I think that's why I end up in trouble so much."

This story that her period linked to her anger had also appeared in her boyfriend's narratives about her. This boyfriend had once called my office and said, "You know how Linda is during her period, right?," as if to establish that Linda's "crazy" behavior while menstruating had become a commonly shared story both in and out of therapy. This belief in the gendered and bodily nature of Linda's mental instability also appeared when Linda faced other kinds of stressors as well. When she nearly lost her house for not making payments on time, she blamed this misfortune on her menstrual status. When she felt passively suicidal after her breakup with her boyfriend, she believed this stemmed from her having PMS. Menstruation became a catchall for her anxieties and problems, a bucket into which she dumped her "unladylike" and disruptive behavior of rebelliousness, anger, troublemaking, and aggression. Once, after dramatically firing me as her therapist (something she did once but never again), she declared during her subsequent apology that this behavior happened because of her period.

In these examples, Linda's borderline personality disorder tendencies and her clearly manic states interfaced with her menstrual cycle in meaningful ways, as menstruation became the funnel through which all negative consequences in her life flowed. Efforts to deconstruct that narrative proved fruitful in her treatment. By working through the ways she actually felt anger (not just at her ex-husband, ex-boyfriends, and her father but also at others), she could better accept that her anger had roots in life experiences rather than merely existing within and because of her body. After getting in touch with her need to express anger, Linda also drew more sustained links between her sex and money habits—as she often had one-night stands and overspent money—and her personal history of being perpetually out of control during her sexual abuse. By *unworking* her narrative around her menstrual cycle, we could better understand and assess her feelings about loss, trauma, and shame, ultimately leaving her with better tools to control and understand her anger while continuing along the long road to recovery. While her "menstrual revolts" did allow her to express anger, redirecting her narratives about that anger toward current and past relationships and traumas helped to actually alleviate her symptoms of depression, mania, and self-destruction.

Moira

Moira, a thirty-eight-year-old, currently separated white woman with three teenage sons, entered therapy for help managing her emotions about her pending divorce. Having recently ended a long-term extra-marital affair, she decided to separate from her husband and initiate divorce proceedings. Moira struggled with depression, lack of self-confidence, poor body image, and feelings of low self-worth. She imagined herself as unlovable and unworthy of love and had begun, following her separation, a series of one-night stands where she engaged in high-risk sexual contact with a variety of men she met on Craigslist. Moira's history revealed long-term family instability and difficulty with body image that extended back into her early childhood. Her father had left the family when Moira was a small girl and had only occasionally appeared in her life via random phone calls, birthday gifts, and (now) Facebook check-ins. She otherwise had no contact with him. Moira's mother, on the other hand, was left to raise her and her sister, often with little financial support, resulting in inconsistent parenting and high conflict during Moira's teenage years. Moira recalled with great distress that her mother would often remark that she would never be beautiful and that she would never make anything of herself.

Struggling to not internalize her mother's views about her lack of beauty and general worthlessness, Moira worked for two years in therapy to improve her body image and work on understanding how her parents had affected her life. Anxious about approaching forty, Moira had expressed some desire to obtain plastic surgery, as she believed that her face started to look too old and her wrinkles had made her profoundly unhappy. Moira, who regularly mentioned her menstrual cycle, believed that only women could understand what she went through and that, even though she dated men and had been married for over fifteen years, she still never felt that men fully understood her. In therapy, she frequently made comments about our alliance as menstruating women, saying comments like, "You know how it is," or "I'm sure you've been there before," or "You know how hard it is to have cramps at work." Her assertions of menstrual solidarity and similarity with me—despite my never speaking directly about my own cycle—demonstrated affinity between us and deepened her connection to me as the (approving, affirming) nurturing figure in her life.

Moira's fear of aging also extended into a paradoxical fear of no longer menstruating. Though she claimed to dislike menstruating, often because it elicited for her feelings of sadness and loneliness, she also felt that it represented her youthfulness and her ability to have children. With her three sons growing older and no longer needing her in the same way as they once did, she now faced conflicts surrounding how to find a new identity in her post-childrearing years while also holding on to her youthfulness. She simultaneously wanted to have her period every month and hated when it arrived. She yearned for its symbolic meaning but ultimately hated the reality of menstruating. Moira enjoyed the reminder that she could still, if she wanted, have children, though she disliked the sadness and panic that often accompanied her cycle. In our work, when I challenged her to think about her sadness and panic as perhaps a grieving process about losing her maternal status, she immediately began to cry and noted that she "always wanted to have little boys" and "missed when they needed me as babies."

As a notable defining moment in her treatment, Moira also began having one-night stands *not* with men her age (as she had done in the past) but with much younger men. She began seeking out men in their early twenties, particularly men who did not have close relationships with their own mothers and who needed some caregiving. Moira expressed deep sexual satisfaction from connecting emotionally and sexually with these younger men who were, by her reports, only a few years older than her sons. She described in detail the vigorous sex they had, the athleticism of their bodies, and her profound satisfaction at feeling recognized as a mother and validated as a sexy and desirable sexual object.

Despite these sexual conquests, Moira continued to describe her emotional life as largely devoted to her female friendships and to our therapeutic relationship. As much of our work focused on her finding independence and self-reliance after years of a (dependent) marriage, Moira worked hard on her artistic endeavors and started her own creative writing business while still keeping her day job working for the city. One day, she came into the office and cried immediately, saying that she had started her period that day and that she felt "so alone, so alone." For Moira, menstruation allowed her the space to feel and express sadness, mostly around themes of aloneness and loss as she struggled to survive on her own financially and emotionally. We ended our work that session with a revelation that menstruation connected her to her (disapproving) mother by reminding her that her mother's menstrual cycle had allowed her to give birth to Moira; ultimately, this had haunted her understanding of menstruation and had presented her with enormous conflict about its meaning and significance. If Moira embraced menstruation, this allowed her to keep her maternal status, but it also reminded her of the implied closeness and connection to her mother. If she distanced herself from her menstrual cycle, she felt the pangs of aging but also felt more disconnected from her mother's disapproval. Remembering her teenage years at all, particularly around the time that she had started menstruating, evoked the traumatic memories of her mother's profound disapproval. By working with Moira to resolve this, and to focus on her own needs and her own definitions of self, her menstrual cycle became, symbolically, a way to process past trauma and to allow for healing from a difficult past.

Blood on the Couch

Ultimately, these three women's disclosures about their menstrual cycles while in therapy showcase the varying utility of menstrual discourse within the trajectory of psychotherapy, particularly as women struggle to understand the connection between their bodies and emotions. In addition to the fascinating connections women make between their own menstrual cycles and their *therapist's* understanding of menstruation (e.g., I have rarely had patients who can imagine that I feel differently about menstrual periods than they do, again revealing that menstrual solidarity also carries assumptions about similarity and shared experiences), they also discussed menstruation as a story that connected their teenage years to their adult lives. Eliciting stories about women's early menstrual experiences can often help to link the patient's experiences of their bodies with their own family histories (e.g., tendencies toward secretiveness versus openness in the family), as these vivid descriptions of starting to menstruate can provide useful connections between adult and childhood years in the context of therapy. Menstrual stories allow the patient and therapist to dig deeply into the past and to unearth relevant details about the family, the body, and the making of the self.

While these three women attached menstruation to strong emotional narratives of shame, anger, and sadness—clearly seeing their periods as a source of personal distress—they also used their menstrual cycles as part of their healing process and, to some extent, as a mode of resistance. This fits well with the notion that, while most women have discussed PMS as a "sickness," some women learn to see these cyclic changes in a more positive light through reframing of the menstrual cycle experience (Lee 2002). It also fits with research showing that women who believe in menstrual distress tend to report much stronger negative symptoms than those who do not already believe in menstrual distress (McFarland, Ross, and DeCourville 1989). Menstrual distress may also have social elements, as women in one study who heard another person talking positively about menstruation did better on an intellectual task (Wister, Stubbs, and Shipman 2013), just as women in lesbian relationships had better attitudes about menstruation than women in heterosexual relationships with men who did not talk about menstruation (Ussher and Perz 2008). Therapy can serve as a key space for reframing, unpacking, and analyzing women's menstrual stories, lessening the self-loathing and disgust women feel toward menstruation, and it can also construct new connections between menstrual distress and other kinds of distress (Roberts and Waters 2004).

Conversations about menstruation can foreground a variety of central themes in the therapy room, particularly about family, emotions, and bodies. At times, even the mere utterance of patients outing themselves as menstruating served as an act of rebellion against a conservative and controlling upbringing (Rosie), while for Moira, her period reminded her of the need to break free from her mother's cruel characterization of her as deficient and ugly. Talking about menstruation during therapy can also provide an avenue to express and experience women's anger in a nonthreatening context, as women often construct anger *because of* menstruation as far less troubling than anger *directed toward* people who have hurt or wronged them. Being "crazy" or out of control in relation to the body/hormones has different implications than expressing that anger as a result of gendered inequalities, oppression, or trauma experienced in relation to others. By starting with menstrual anger and moving to anger about these broader themes like inequalities and trauma, women can get in touch with their outrage about other painful aspects of their lives. Clearly, the use of, and discussion about, menstruation during psychotherapy can illuminate the often fragile links women have between their adulthood and childhood, body and mind, emotions and thoughts, and their traumatized and rebellious selves.

9

The Menstruating Male Body

Trans bodies and trans lives have increasingly occupied space both within academic feminism (e.g., gender studies courses, feminist conferences, special issues of journals) and within the popular media. Necessary theorizing about the provocative role of trans bodies in the corpus of feminist theory (MacDonald 1998; Stryker, Currah, and Moore 2008) alongside the interrogation of the tangible stressors and terrors of trans lives (Levitt and Ippoliti 2013) have thrust trans identities into the forefront of academic feminist theory. For example, clear articulations about the inclusion or exclusion of trans women from "women only" spaces have appeared as a major rift in conceptualizations of modern feminism. Whether "women only" spaces include only women-born women, or whether they should also include trans women, has recently made headlines, particularly as radical feminists and factions of the trans community clash about the meaning and role of trans bodies (Goldberg 2014). However, while feminist theory has developed increasingly sophisticated and complex ways of imagining and theorizing trans bodies and identities, psychotherapy work, on the other hand, lags behind in the assessment and articulation of trans client experiences and needs.

Psychotherapy work on trans clients and trans identities has only recently begun to address the need for understanding the developmental, psychological, social, and relational needs of trans clients. A continued insistence on diagnosing all transgender clients as having "gender identity disorder" (and such diagnoses are currently required in order to obtain any health insurance coverage of trans surgeries and hormone therapies) falsely frames trans identities as necessarily pathological (McLachlan and Lindegger 2012; Sallans 2012). Coupled with the reality that many trans clients must modify their gender presentation to secure their safety, or stay closeted at work to avoid losing their jobs, trans identities typically appear in the literature as a severe stressor or frank pathology rather than as a normal or healthy identity (Levitt and Ippoliti 2013).

Surprisingly little psychological work has refuted the positioning of trans identities as pathological, dangerous, or even monstrous (Leite 2012), though some work has started to examine the more affirming dimensions of trans lives. For example, the focus on transgender identity affirmation, particularly helping trans clients to disclose their identities and gain recognition as trans, has formed a key part of the emerging literature on trans therapies (Nuttbrock, Rosenblum, and Blumenstein 2002). Activists have lobbied to have "gender identity disorder" removed from the DSM and have argued that requiring psychotherapy in order to obtain a letter of support for hormone therapy limits the meaningful work that could transpire between therapist and trans client (Sallans 2012). Depth therapy, a form of psychodynamic psychotherapy, has yielded success as one possible long-term technique for trans therapies, but it requires more than a short-term, health insurance–based investment for such work (Fraser 2009). Trans clients, for example, typically present to therapy with a range of goals: understanding and resolving their body-mind dissonance, negotiating and managing their identities, addressing minority stress, and undertaking the process of transitioning (Morgan 2012). Given the greater prevalence of male-to-female (MTF) versus female-to-male (FTM) trans clients, different ways of negotiating gender and treatment goals for FTM and MTF clients are needed in trans therapies (Giami and Beaubatie 2011). Such work typically has positive results, as trans clients who felt more congruence between their gender identity and external appearance reported more life satisfaction and life meaning alongside less anxiety and depression (Kozee, Tylka, and Bauerband 2012).

In my therapy practice, I regularly hear from my trans clients that their previous therapists have overprioritized conversations where trans clients must educate therapists about their needs, lifestyles, surgeries, stressors, and the particulars of "how it works" to live in a trans body. The perceived need to educate counselors and therapists about trans issues is widespread; one study reported that trans patients described this as their biggest problem connected to seeing mental health professionals (Israel et al. 2008). For female-to-male trans men, this has resulted in feelings of isolation, depression, and difficulty in asking for help from therapists, particularly as therapy is often framed as a "feminizing" experience or as something that women more often seek out (Philipson 1993); moreover, therapists typically reward female traits over male traits when assessing success in therapy (Heatherington, Stets, and Mazzarella 1986). Further, trans clients have verbalized how difficult it is to negotiate coming to therapy for the dual purposes of addressing their psychological issues and obtaining support for surgery and hormone therapy. (Legally, trans patients need a supportive letter from a therapist in order to undergo medical treatment to remove their breasts or alter their genitals.) These goals often contrast, as trans clients sometimes feel they cannot tell the truth to therapists because it risks their ability to obtain the necessary diagnoses and treatment support letters they want. Coupled with high rates of trauma, for example, these blocks in dialogue and disclosure present formidable challenges to the patient-therapist relationship (Richmond, Burnes, and Carroll 2012). The complex realities of trans therapies and the unique relationship between the trans client and the therapist (who essentially is tasked with making a decision about whether trans clients can and should medically transition) present a difficult backdrop for optimal therapeutic work.

Though I had not originally intended to specialize in trans therapies, I began several years ago to receive an increasing number of referrals for trans clients (particularly FTM clients) who could not find trans-affirmative therapists where they lived. As a therapist who specializes in sexuality and body issues, the addition of trans clients to my caseload fit nicely with my areas of expertise. After all, trans clients often report distress about their body image, particularly related to not meeting the harsh dichotomized standards of traditional masculinity and femininity (Pfeffer 2008). (Gay and lesbian clients, too, often seek out LGBT-affirming therapists because they have so often encountered therapists with deeply entrenched prejudices and biases about sexual identity; see Liddle 1997.) Since 2010, I have seen dozens of trans men in therapy, many of whom I have treated for longer-term therapies. Within these therapies, the topic of menstruation and its symbolic and literal meaning has been discussed repeatedly and often with much distress for FTM clients.

To date, surprisingly little work has interrogated trans men's experiences of menstruation, particularly within feminist therapy work. A few studies suggest that menstruation matters to FTM patients, but they do not elaborate on just *how* it matters or the specific clinical issues that FTM patients present about their menstrual cycles (Pfeffer 2008; Schleifer 2006). The limited available detailed work on the topic of trans men's menstruation experiences has appeared in more informal places like blogs and Tumblr posts (Reading 2014), leaving a notable gap in academic scholarship on the topic.

This essay highlights my work with three FTM trans men in psychotherapy who initially discussed their menstrual cycles as a source of unhappiness, stress, and, at times, trauma. By unworking essentialist notions of male and female bodies and questioning the inherent meanings and symbolism around menstruation, I outline the complexities of situating menstruation as a signifier of a "gendered self," followed by an articulation of what I see as the transgressive potential in imagining space for menstruating male bodies within feminist politics. Ultimately, trans men's menstrual cycles can serve a powerful literal and metaphorical role in challenging their ideas about masculinity, femininity, cycles, and transitioning.

Nash

Nash, a thirty-six-year-old white FTM trans man, entered therapy as part of a court-ordered anger management program related to explosive outbursts with his wife and a custody battle about his son, Lawrence. Nash had started identifying as trans at age ten and had changed his name to Nash as soon as he turned eighteen; he presented in therapy as friendly, doggedly macho, and relatively uncomfortable talking about his feelings. As a long-haul truck driver for a major transportation company, he worked long hours and reported that he liked the money but did not care much for his job. Nash had developed a technique of urinating while standing up and regularly used the men's room at the various truck stops he routinely visited; he had thus far never been identified as trans by anyone in these truck stop men's rooms, though he constantly feared others discovering his trans identity.

Identifying fully as male and rarely disclosing his trans status to others (he passed with remarkable ease in most public spaces), Nash said that he yearned to have top surgery on his breasts but remained firmly disinterested in bottom surgery on his genitals. In one of our early sessions, Nash described that he "spiritually had a penis" and that he could feel his penis psychologically and sexually during intercourse with his wife. He explained that if he believed enough in the presence of his penis, both he and his wife could feel it. Nash believed that his maleness stemmed from deep within; when talking about this, he referenced Native American two-spirit people and his affinity for that identity.

Despite his acceptance of his "spiritual penis" and his resistance to having bottom surgery, Nash adamantly wanted to have top surgery and to remove his breasts entirely. He had small breasts that he wrapped with extensive Ace bandages; he believed that even without this wrapping most people would not recognize his breasts as female per se (he thought they looked more like a "fat man's boobs"). Still, the demands of his work and the long hours he put in wore him down physically; he wanted one less thing to manage physically. He sought out therapy to process whether the presence of his breasts had caused his anger to worsen and to explore possible psychological implications of having his breasts removed. He had recently had a series of explosive outbursts at his wife when she threatened to leave him, and she retaliated by promising to remove their son (he adopted Lawrence at an early age) if it happened again. Nash saw these outbursts and his feelings about his body as interconnected, and he expressed a frank need for help from "someone who understands what I'm going through."

Nash approached therapy in highly practical terms and spoke quickly—almost frantically—during our sessions together. Nash had taken testosterone injections for years and had nearly perfected the art of speaking as a man; his tone, inflection, and performance of masculinity was unmatched among my trans clients. He showed up to most sessions in visibly dirty boots that flaked mud onto the floor, and he wore smelly clothes that reeked of gasoline and dirt (hazards of his job). His fingernails always had a crust of dirt around them. Nash commented once that his choice to shower infrequently and to wear dirty men's Wranglers helped him feel like a "real man," but he also apologized for getting the couch and floor dirty with his muddy boots. It took several sessions before we could unpack these aesthetic choices and his need to perform masculinity in this way during our sessions.

Over the course of the six months I worked with Nash, the subject of menstruation arose several times, particularly in relation to his vivid descriptions of how much he feared hate crimes. For Nash, menstruation symbolized his pervasive fear of being discovered as biologically female. He described how he typically managed his menstrual cycle by leaving a tampon in for twelve hours at a time (he refused to change tampons at any restroom other than his hotel restroom or sometimes in the back of his truck). Nash spent his entire menstrual cycle hoping not to bleed through, and he constantly feared that other men would hurt or even kill him if they discovered him as FTM. Menstruation felt like a lethal form of "outing" him as a trans man. He reported that he had tried spiritually and psychologically to block himself from menstruating, that he prayed to God regularly for his cycle to stop, and that he loathed and hated himself with great ferocity during his menstrual periods. He could not reconcile his feelings of being male with having a uterus, vagina, vulva, or menstrual period, and he described these conflicts not in academic or theoretical terms but instead by using the language of survival.

For Nash, merely tolerating his menstrual cycle could not sufficiently address the stress and trauma he felt about his menstrual cycle. We approached his negativity about menstruation by using multiple tactics and interventions. First, Nash had never heard of toxic shock syndrome and did not know about any risks of leaving tampons in for twelve or more hours at a time. I suggested that he change over to the DivaCup, a reusable menstrual cup that he could leave in for longer than conventional tampons. We talked about how to insert the cup, care for it, wash it, and use it in private and public spaces. Second, we worked on fundamentally reimagining menstruation as something that he could gender in highly male and masculine terms, much like he had rescripted his vaginal lubrication during sex as "semen" in a spiritual sense. Nash had a strong belief that his mind could impact the physical manifestations of masculinity; short of stopping his menstrual cycle altogether, our work to reframe menstruation as masculine targeted his beliefs, attitudes, and cognitions as well as his emotions.

These approaches to addressing Nash's menstrual needs succeeded to varying degrees. Nash ended up liking the DivaCup and transitioned over to using it instead of tampons almost immediately. He complained that he did not know of its existence prior to starting therapy and that he felt frustrated that no one had ever told him about this method of menstrual management before. He practiced insertion and removal techniques privately for his first cycle and quickly figured out how to manage the cup while working on the road or while at home. (He also feared that his young son would discover that he was "not a real Dad" if evidence of menstrual blood or menstrual products were left at the house.)

In terms of working on the psychological and spiritual feelings he had about menstruation, Nash and I worked for months on how to masculinize his menstrual periods. He talked about menstrual blood as his body trying to get rid of his uterus (not anatomically or biologically true, of course, but he conceptualized it this way). In this sense, he reframed menstruation as his ally in ridding himself of his feminized womb. Nash also talked about how he did *not* feel more feminine when he connected to his emotions about his son and how, if he could see himself as a good father, he could also see his menstrual cycle as "just something that happened to me." He thought deeply and talked openly about how much men bleed (and how blood is associated with masculinity) in mainstream Hollywood movies, describing his menstrual blood as a "war wound" and "something I can get through." In sum, Nash devoted great effort to reframing menstruation within the framework of traditional masculinity.

Notably, Nash did not want to see himself as genderqueer, partially trans, in transition, or anything in the middle of the gender binary. For Nash, "being male" meant being fully and exclusively male. Thus, he felt more at peace with his menstrual cycle when he used a product that better protected his secretive trans identity from others in public restrooms and when he reframed menstruation (and menstrual blood) as related to traditionally masculine things: war, fatherhood, and the expulsion of his womanliness/womb. By harnessing his tendency to cognitively challenge ideas about his own genitals (his "spiritual penis"), this reframe built upon work he had already done to undo the biological inevitability of his body and its meanings. Further, Nash's therapy work demonstrated the importance of not only challenging gender binaries by imagining gender as in flux (or as fluid)—something that seems helpful to some trans patients but less helpful to others—but also by actively working to help trans male patients to infuse their own somewhat rigid definitions of maleness and masculinity with new conceptualizations of male sexualities, bodies, and identities. Nash had to create a masculinized menstrual experience that retained his self-image as fully male.

Ty

Ty, a twenty-four-year-old biracial African American/white trans man, presented for therapy with distress about his body, problems with depression and self-destructive tendencies, and a desire to start testosterone hormone therapy. Overweight and often unkempt, Ty had struggled with depression for many years and sometimes felt passively suicidal; he had begun cutting himself two years ago while in high school and had recently broken up with his (heterosexual identified) girlfriend. Most of his other relationships occurred online through various gaming sites like World of Warcraft, and he rarely had contact with people outside of his job at a local restaurant. Ty had started identifying as male a year ago and had recently come out to his religious and conservative family; they had reacted to the news of Ty's trans identity by consigning him to "a life of Hell" and strongly proclaiming it as "just a phase." His aunt had chided him as "gay but not admitting it," and his mother believed that trans and gay identities happened because gay priests had recruited people to the gay lifestyle. Ty worked hard to embrace his trans identity and to believe he could endure the hardships that such a life would entail, though he also knew that getting top surgery, starting hormones, and living as a male constituted "a dream that seemed too far away."

When Ty started therapy, he wore large baggy sweatshirts, cut his hair short, and adopted a punk aesthetic complete with dyed black hair, nose rings, ear gauges, and various chains around his neck. He described a variety of ongoing stressors related to money issues, aloneness, constantly feeling unable to support himself, underemployment, body image problems, religious conflicts both with others and within himself, and a near-permanent sense that he had "no way out." He had, for a time, considered going into the military but faced the reality that trans identities would pose a threat to the traditional sorts of masculinity required in the military and that he would not earn others' acceptance as a trans man. Ty also assumed that his dreams of going to college would never come to fruition, both because of his limited finances and because his family described going to college as "frivolous and worthless."

Several weeks into the therapy, Ty started to mention his menstrual cycle with increasing regularity, citing his irregular periods as a "gift from God" and saying that when he had his period, he would shower for a full hour to clean himself. Ty believed that his irregular periods were "a sign" that God made him male. He talked about his vagina and vulva as "down there" and rolled his eyes whenever he looked down at his body during session. Ty felt resolutely opposed to any positive emotions about his menstrual cycle and expressed certainty that someday he would rid himself of it permanently. Any efforts to help him make peace with bleeding—by constructing it as temporary, nonthreatening, or possibly masculine—had failed. He told me that he wanted to rip out his uterus and that he "could not be the person I was meant to be" as long as he bled.

Several months later, we talked about what sort of man he wanted to be after he completed his transition. Ty described his ideal masculinity as, surprisingly, quite traditionally feminine. He wanted to provide financial support and physical protection to his partner (more traditionally masculine), but he also wanted to cry, express emotional connection, bond with his partner and their children, and "spoil" his partner with love, affection, and gifts. He admitted, for the first time, that he did not want to have bottom surgery and that "keeping my parts intact" would allow him to stay emotional and connected to others. He believed that removing or tampering with his uterus or "girl parts" would strip him of the ability to maintain emotional connections with his future partner and their future children. The gender binary, in short, had not totally absorbed his feminine self.

Using this gender fluidity as a basis, we worked on ways to imagine his menstrual cycle as also a part of his emotional connection to the world. Ty admitted that when he menstruated he often cried more and felt more in tune with others' feelings; building upon this, he said that he could maybe see his menstrual period as helping him to "keep it real, emotionally." For Ty, being feminine *and* having a male identity could perhaps coincide, as long as he identified as male, used the male pronoun, had top surgery, took testosterone, and successfully convinced others to see and acknowledge him as male. He said, poignantly, "If other people call me a man, then I can keep the parts of me that are a woman."

Ultimately, Ty also started to question his traditional beliefs about gender, particularly his belief that providing financially for a partner constituted good or appropriate masculinity. Over the course of therapy, he decided instead that he would like a more egalitarian partnership with someone, one where they both had jobs and both took care of each other. He also reported that his body image had improved and that he felt more sexual and more in tune with his sexual desires. Though he still fantasized that he would eventually stop menstruating altogether, he nevertheless talked about his relief when he could "finally cry" during his period. For Ty, admitting that the traditionally feminine body did not feel entirely repulsive or negative constituted a major step toward accepting his current in-between male and female trans body. He also recognized that he could divorce his physical body from the emotional characteristics associated with men and women or, in the case of menstruation, could use his physical body to experience *both* his masculine and feminine selves.

Scott

Scott, an eighteen-year-old white trans male, had initially entered a four-year-long period of therapy at age fourteen during the summer before he started high school. He presented with symptoms of anxiety and depression related to his inability to feel fully masculine. His father, a single dad struggling to make ends meet for him and his younger sister, placed him in therapy because his mood had deteriorated and he had become agitated and defiant about his gender identity. His father wanted him to be happy, accepted his decision to call himself a boy, and wanted to support him in any way possible. His estranged mother, whom Scott only saw on rare occasion, refused to acknowledge Scott as her son and said that she "gave birth to a girl and Scott was a girl." Scott had started calling himself a boy and using the male pronoun a few months prior to starting high school, but at that time had not yet gone through puberty. He stated as his goal for therapy: "I want people in high school to think I'm a boy."

Scott generally presented with stable mental health and a positive outlook about his friendships and his relationship with his father and sister. He reported that he had quite a few friends in school and that kids at school thought it was "cool" that he identified as trans. He had grown increasingly uneasy about the possibility of starting high school as a trans male and instead wanted to "pass as a guy, not a trans guy." He had recently started his period and had also started to grow breasts, both of which threatened his idea of the masculinity he so desperately wanted to cultivate. He fantasized about having a "straight girlfriend who will like me because I'm a guy," and he wanted to grow muscles and have a stronger, more robust physical appearance.

When talking specifically about menstruation, Scott described his first period as the single most horrifying experience of his life. He had learned about menstruation in school but did not anticipate what it would feel like to menstruate, especially when he realized that he would have to use tampons or pads to manage his period. Because his father had largely ignored the topic and his mother never discussed it with him, Scott felt wholly underprepared to handle the stress of menstruation. He described feeling ashamed of using the men's restroom at school to change his pads, but he said that the kids at school made fun of him when went into the women's restroom. To address these tensions, he had punched several boys at school and had gotten into three fistfights during the last month of eighth grade. During high school, Scott felt intent upon controlling his anger and "starting to become a guy as soon as possible."

After Scott started high school and tried to identify exclusively as male, he reported with distress that others could see that he wore breast binders and that most schoolmates knew Scott had been born female. He had started dating a girl in his class, but her parents felt uncomfortable with their daughter "being a lesbian" and had forbade further contact. Scott repeatedly exclaimed, "I just want to be a guy!" I responded in one of our sessions by explaining that there were many other categories besides male and female and that he might take comfort in examining the many options for labeling and identities. We talked about the difference between gender identity (one's self-identified gender) and sexual identity (one's sexual interest in others) along with the meaning of words and phrases like "gender fluidity," "homoromantic," "pansexual," and "genderqueer." Scott's face lit up with excitement and he told me that he was definitely "genderqueer."

Over the next several weeks he settled into a new understanding of his body and his identity, telling me that "genderqueer" made more sense while he waited for hormones, surgery, and "the rest of my life to happen." Kids at school admired him for identifying as "genderqueer" and he liked explaining this definition to them. After researching online about "genderqueer" identities, Scott decided that he felt more comfortable in the middle of two genders or without a gender at all. During this process, he also became more comfortable with his menstrual cycle, allowing his period to merge with his conceptualization of someone who identified as "genderqueer." (That said, he stopped using the restrooms at school entirely, often holding in his urine for eight hours at a time and refusing to drink much water during the morning or throughout the day.) For Scott, learning about and embracing new categories of identity aside from only male or female allowed him to accept the aspects of his teenage body that were becoming female (particularly breasts and menstruation), just as he could embrace the possibilities of his masculinity that went beyond fighting and grandstanding. For example, Scott and his dad took up hunting and fishing so that he could express himself more "as a guy." Implicitly, Scott's therapy work around menstruation demonstrated the critical importance of expanding the queer identity circle to include as many different variations of gender and sexual identities as possible, while also showing the very real psychological consequences of moving into a more middle space of gender. Scott's menstrual narratives could more closely align with his emerging postpubescent body when he embraced the middle spaces of gender and sexual identity.

Making Space for the Menstruating Male Body

While all three of these cases clearly have different implications for masculinity, menstruation, and trans identities, they collectively reveal how therapy work that focuses on undoing binary notions of male and female bodies can powerfully resituate the implied meanings of and symbolism around menstruation. If trans male clients can reimagine menstruation as having different meanings beyond the "failing" male body, they can also work to make peace with the aspects of their bodies and identities that remain (and may always remain) attached to the stereotypically or traditionally female. If menstrual cycles become less threatening, so too might vaginas, uteruses, vulvas, and breasts; further, the traits that trans men see within themselves (e.g., Ty's descriptions of emotionality) may also be expressed more freely and abundantly. These three cases highlight the importance of reconciling multiple coexisting genders, integrating masculine and feminine selves, and allowing room for reconciliation between distal points on the gender binary.

These cases also vividly show the distance between those who can take shelter within the more academic or theoretical aspects of trans identity (e.g., Scott's enjoyment and embrace of the descriptor "genderqueer") compared to those who live largely without such protections (e.g., Nash's fears of being murdered in a bathroom at a truck stop). Understanding the menstruating male body, then, also connects deeply to the ways that trans men are understood and viewed. For those (like Scott) coming of age in fairly progressive high schools, less direct and overt hostility and more subtle barriers to full equality may be faced. For those living within more traditional and conservative communities, trans male identities may pose a greater threat to the existing social order and may elicit more fear, hostility, and even violence from others. Menstruation, then, becomes a space of both practical, physical management—for example, how to find a product that will allow absorption of menstrual blood for twelve hours or longer—and it relates to the symbolic and metaphorical weight of the menstruating male body. Such complicated terrain, particularly within a therapy office, can lead to fruitful and productive directions for trans men to explore about themselves.

Menstruating male bodies have transgressive potential both within psychotherapy and within feminist politics more broadly, particularly as notions of "the biological" fade away (Johnston-Robledo and Stubbs 2013). Tensions between bodies and sexualities as utilitarian/practical versus abstract/theoretical can appear vividly in a therapy office, as a patient's distress echoes loudly against the backdrop of gender and feminist theory. For example, how can therapists avoid imposing their own frameworks of gender and sexual identity while simultaneously challenging trans patients to critically examine their own bodies? How can psychotherapy work move beyond the mere assessment of so-called "pathology" and instead prioritize trans patients' narratives of the body and self?

Ultimately, by examining psychotherapy work with menstruating men, the biological and supposedly "natural" process of menstruation, vividly remade in the male body, gives way instead to a rebellious, multigendered, and defiant experience for both male- and female-bodied people. The menstrual narratives of trans men truly exemplify the importance of queering menstruation and making space for nonessentialist modes of imagining menstruation. As these three examples show, many menstruating trans men have engaged in work to understand, unpack, and undo their ties to the inevitable and "natural" body in ways that exemplify the powerful social justice implications of deconstructing binaries and promoting a social-constructionist per-spective in psychotherapy.

Part Four

Menarchy and Menstrual Activism

10

Raising Bloody Hell

Inciting Menstrual Panics through Campus and Community Activism

Introduction

When I teach a course called Gender, Bodies, and Health, designed to explore topics that include everything from pregnancy and domestic violence to orgasm and food politics, nothing provokes more disgust, hostility, and discomfort than the week on menstruation. Male students have left the class on the first day when I merely mention that we will study menstruation in the second week; women often gaze uncomfortably down at the syllabus and have later characterized menstruation as a topic they *do not discuss.* Certainly, the panics that surround menstruation have long rendered the menstruating body shameful, taboo, silent, and even pathological. From the historic separation of women's menstruating bodies into "menstrual huts" (Guterman, Mehta, and Gibbs 2008) to the pervasive insistence upon the (pre)menstruating body as disordered (e.g., PMDD, accusations of women "on the rag" when they express anger, etc.), women have had to confront their internalized body shame and cultural expectations for the *absence* of menstruation for some time.

This chapter examines complex responses to a simple activism assignment given to students in my Psychology of Gender course in which I asked undergraduates to design a public intervention that would challenge negative attitudes about menstruation. By examining the history of menstrual shame and, conversely, menstrual *activism* to combat such shame, along with an account of the kinds of strategic interventions students created, I outline the relationship between gender, power, and the menstruating body. I then explore the potential volatility surrounding the moral panics of menstruation by reflecting on the unexpected moral panic that ensued following the completion of this assignment.

"Managing" Menstrual Shame

Women's bodies in their "natural" state have long elicited particular disdain, as routine processes of the body—growing body hair, sweating during exercise, breastfeeding in public, having natural body odors, weight gain, menstruating each month—have become more tightly controlled, monitored, and, in some cases, *eliminated* by the ever-narrowing cultural ideas of womanhood. Women routinely engage in a variety of normative body practices that manage and hide their "disgusting" bodies (Roberts and Goldenberg 2007), whether shaving their entire bodies (Fahs 2011a; Tiggemann and Lewis 2004), avoiding exercise altogether or wearing "sexy" exercise clothes, breastfeeding only in private and behind closed doors, using beauty products to mask their natural scents, or hiding tampons and pads. While women struggle in general with accepting their bodies as "leaky" and "viscous," menstruation signifies a particularly painful union between cultural narratives of menstruation as shameful combined with women's own experiences of menstruation as taboo (Mansfield and Stubbs 2007).

When women worry about revealing their "menstrual status," they tap into a long history of panics surrounding menstruation. Historically, women learned to see menstruation as taboo and as something in need of *management* (Delaney, Lupton, and Toth 1988), as menstrual blood implied disease, social violations, and spiritual corruption (Read 2008; Shuttle and Redgrove 1988). Western narratives of menstruation today treat it as failed reproduction (Kerkham 2003) in large part because the state treats women's bodies as machines of reproduction (Martin 2001). Still, even though disdain permeates cultural and patriarchal attitudes toward menstruation, some cultures (particularly African tribes) value menstruation, sometimes even simulating it as a powerful and revered practice (Brain 1988).

Overwhelmingly, women (especially *young* women) face an onslaught of images and ideas that treat menstruation as disgusting, tainting, and even frankly disabling; such narratives promote the idea that a woman's period could paralyze her from her participation in sports, career, or family life. Negative rhetoric surrounding menstruation has also circulated as justification for preventing women from becoming president or holding serious positions of power. The surge in menstrual suppression products (e.g., the oral contraceptive Seasonale, which creates four periods a year, or Lybrel, which eliminates all periods) portrays the *nonmenstruating* body as ideal and of ultimate cultural value (Johnston-Robledo, Barnack, and Wares 2006; Rose, Chrisler, and Couture 2008). Similarly, when selling disposable menstrual products, advertisers depict the menstruating female body as unclean, unfeminine, and dirty in order to effectively market panty liners, pads, and tampons (Berg and Coutts 1994; Kissling 2006). In these mainstream advertisements, little acknowledgment of the environmental consequences of disposable, one-time-use pads and tampons enter the equation, thus promoting hyperconsumerism and teaching women to see menstruation as taboo (Davidson 2012). The phrase *feminine hygiene*—a relic from the 1930s advertisements for birth control—still suggests the dirtiness of the natural female body and the relative "cleanliness" women can aspire to when using menstrual products (Fahs 2012b; Tone 1996). (Notably, alternative or ecofriendly products like Lunapads, GladRags, and the DivaCup avoid *feminine hygiene* references and instead use more straight-forward terminology like *menstruation* and *cycle*; see http://lunapads.com/). Additionally, films that portray menstruation overwhelmingly depict the "horrors" of menstruation or, more narrowly, the basic coming-of-age moments girls experience with the onset of their first menstrual cycle (Briefel 2005; Kissling 2002; Rosewarne 2012), largely ignoring menstruation as a normative and *adult* process.

Girls face particularly negative messages about menstruation and learn early on to dislike their menstruating bodies, particularly for older girls (Rembeck, Moller, and Gunnarsson 2006), those prone to self-objectification (Roberts and Waters 2004), those with more body shame and less sexual experience (Schooler et al. 2005), those with negativity toward breastfeeding (Johnston-Robledo et al. 2007), and those who communicated with their mothers less often about menstruation (Rembeck, Moller, and Gunnarsson 2006). As adults, the menstrual taboo often continues, particularly within women's sexual relationships. Less than half of women in one study engaged in menstrual sex, and over 30 percent of women said they would *never* have menstrual sex (Allen and Goldberg 2009). Further, heterosexual-identified women felt far more negatively toward menstrual sex than did lesbians or bisexual women (even if they had male partners) (Fahs 2011b).

"Raising critical consciousness": Menstrual Anarchy and Embodied Rebellion

Despite, or perhaps *because of*, the overwhelming negativity and disgust directed toward menstruation, feminists, environmentalists, and other activists have fought back. In Shannon Docherty's (2010) aptly titled article "Smear it on your face, rub it on your body, it's time to start a menstrual party!," the direct confrontational tone of menstrual activism comes across clearly. Menstrual activists—first appearing in the second wave and also known as "menarchists"—have responded to negative portrayals of menstruation by using media campaigns, consciousness-raising, educational campaigns, and assaults on mainstream representations of menstruation. In addition to depathologizing menstruation and fighting against PMS and PMDD (Chrisler 2007), they have fought against toxic menstrual products that use chemicals that harm the vaginal lining (Bobel 2006), brought a critical voice to menstrual-suppression products (Johnston-Robledo, Barnack, and Wares 2006), and encouraged women to develop more positive feelings about menstruation by seeing it as affirming of womanhood, a sign of nonpregnancy, and a symbol of overall health and well-being (Bobel 2010; Kissling 2006; Stubbs and Costos 2004). Rather than seeing menstruation as something to keep hidden, menstrual activists advocate for more education about menses and more discussion and openness about menstruation in health settings, classrooms, and family life (Kissling 2006).

Most importantly, menstrual activists want both men and women to develop a stronger and more nuanced critical consciousness about the social context for menstruation, particularly the shame narratives directed at women's bodies (Bobel 2008, 2010). Menstrual activists strive for more positive representations of menstruation along with safer products and more comprehensive, honest, and forthcoming dialogue about women's menstruating bodies (Bobel 2010). From advocating herbal remedies for cramps (Blood Sisters 2010) to celebrating the power of the "cunt" (Carpenter 2009), to showcasing connections between the personal and the political (Society for Menstrual Cycle Research), to teaching women to track and understand their cycles in an irreverent and humorous way (Quint 2009), activists have made many meaningful and diverse interventions. As Chris Bobel (2010) writes, "Menstrual activism rejects the construction of menstruation as a problem in need of a solution. . . . The study of menstrual activism yields important insights into the evolution of social movements and feminist epistemology, a system of knowledges in constant flux" (7). More specifically, menstrual activists question why many women hate their periods more than their other bodily processes, and they interrogate the ways that culture, gender ideology, and consumerism have shaped these reactions (Bobel 2010).

Menstrual activists also emphasize that everyday acts of deviance—resisting commercial pads and tampons, injecting menstruation into public discourse, consuming less television—have particular relevance for resisting mainstream ideologies of menstruation and patriarchy, as "activists" need not form a singular, organized body (Bobel 2007). Thus, menstrual activism represents an ideal site of resistance for *new* activists, particularly undergraduate students, those consciously confronting sexism for the first time, and budding feminists.

Consciousness-Raising in the Classroom

> Justice must always question itself, just as society can exist only by means of the work it does on itself and its institutions.
>
> —Michel Foucault, *Libération*

As most people adamantly claim (much to the chagrin of feminist critics) that they have complete control over the decisions they make with their body (Gill 2007), the task of motivating undergraduates to question the *agency* of their bodily choices provides a formidable challenge to women's studies instructors. Teaching students to imagine their bodies as sites of political, social, gendered, and cultural conflicts—often waged *at their expense*—represents a central goal of a women's studies education. As students sometimes dismiss women's studies course content as irrelevant to their lives (Webber 2005) or become outright hostile and critical of women's studies instructors (Hartung 1990; Stake and Hoffmann 2000), feminist educators must negotiate difficult and provocative classroom environments that yield diverse responses from students on a regular basis. That said, studies have shown that students also benefit greatly from taking women's studies courses, reporting a more progressive gender role orientation, less prejudice toward women, more agency and control over their lives, more support for affirmative action, greater involvement in the women's movement, more activism, and more identification with feminism compared to students who did not take such courses (Bryant 2003; Harris, Melaas, and Rodacker 1999; Henderson-King and Stewart 1999; Stake 2007; Stake et al. 1994).

As the feminist classroom serves as an ideal space for challenging power (Maher 1999), confronting sexist and racist institutions (Enns and Sinacore 2004), and helping students to develop a critical consciousness that links up with their personal experiences (Fahs 2011a; Stake and Hoffmann 2000), activist interventions should form a central part of the women's studies curriculum. Still, feminist professors often shy away from integrating experiential forms of activism directly into the course curriculum and far too rarely use consciousness-raising exercises and assignments (Enns and Sinacore 2004), even though students benefit most from experiential assignments that prioritize reflection and "applied feminism" rather than cataloguing facts, passive learning, and less "hands-on" assignments (Copp and Kleinman 2008).

Given the significance of menstrual activism, its relevance to *new* activists, and the importance of linking activism to the feminist classroom experience, I embarked upon a new assignment in the fall 2011 semester at Arizona State University in my upper-division, cross-listed psychology and women and gender studies course entitled Psychology of Gender. The class of forty students included mostly those under age thirty, roughly 25 percent male students and 75 percent female students, and a vastly diverse range of races and sexual identities. This assignment, dubbed the "menstrual activism project," asked students to form groups of five to seven students where they would: 1) Strategize and identify a priority area that they would like to see changed in contemporary attitudes toward menstruation (e.g., availability of menstrual products, attitudes toward menstrual sex, men's attitudes toward purchasing menstrual products, advertisements that construct the nonmenstruating body as "normal," and so on); 2) Devise an activist intervention that would combat this negative norm, though it must be manageable in scope and potentially enacted either on campus or in the broader community; 3) Enact this intervention and record the results (e.g., photos, videotaping, interviews); 4) Write a paper on the activist project using relevant research on menstruation; and 5) Present the activist project to the class and at the Moral Panics of Sexuality conference. I framed the assignment as an introduction to activism and encouraged students to think creatively and critically about how they would like to intervene about negative menstrual attitudes.

With this prompt, six student groups created activism projects that spanned a wide range of ideas and tactics. One group labeled hundreds of menstrual products with accurate information about the menstrual cycle and handed out the products all throughout campus to both male and female students. They also made posters, affixed tampons to the posters, and placed them in "high-density" areas like the student cafeteria and the main classroom buildings. A second group targeted the safety and toxicity of tampons and devised a campus intervention for raising awareness about the dangers of tampons by using posters, interviews, and fliers about REDSCAM. A third group created a Facebook page to measure people's attitudes about buying menstrual products and then distributed buttons to men on campus and in the community that read, boldly, *Real Men Buy Tampons!* They filmed these reactions and documented people's responses to men wearing the buttons.

A fourth group entered gas stations and set up a box of free tampons at each counter with a brightly colored Japanese anime character called Period Girl stuck to the top of the box. They then filmed people's reactions—ranging from gratitude for the free supplies to outright hostility and outrage—at each gas station store. A fifth group made signs that said, "Honk if you like sex during menstruation" and stood at three locations—the corner of campus, a mall, and near a community center—to assess differences in responses. Finally, a sixth group staged a scene where a female actor, accompanied by a "friend," wore white pants with a noticeable but realistic-looking menstrual stain on them and walked through the mall while another student clandestinely filmed people's reactions. If anyone approached the actor to tell her about the leak, she handed them a flier and explained the intervention.

In student papers and class presentations after these interventions, students expressed a variety of reactions and emotions about their activist projects. Prior to starting the assignment, many students felt menstrual activism would be "no big deal" and would not generate much excitement or interest. After doing the assignment, nearly all students reported, in their papers and presentations, feeling shocked and outraged by the degree of negativity they encountered from others, particularly men and university officials, when engaging in the assignment. When distributing tampons, many men would not touch the products and some people labeled the group members as disgusting. One university administrator removed the tampon-decorated sign from the cafeteria, saying it was "inappropriate for an eating environment." While people reacted less negatively to the group raising awareness about the potential toxicity of tampons, this group also encountered stares, avoidance, and anger that they had raised the issue publicly. The group distributing the *Real Men Buy Tampons!* buttons also noticed a large range of responses: some men eagerly took the buttons and wore them proudly, while most expressed disdain, denial, and hostility at the idea that they *should* feel comfortable buying tampons.

While the campus interventions certainly provoked a range of responses, including a variety of negative reactions, the community interventions provoked even more direct and aggressive responses from others. The gas station intervention offended many of the gas station attendants, who yelled at the women to "get out of here!" No box of free supplies lasted long and all were eventually removed. The menstrual sex intervention, as we later found out, provoked one of the harshest responses from the community. While some cars drove by and happily honked their horns, others rolled up their windows and refused to make eye contact, and still others believed the posters signified the "deviance" of the university itself. The final intervention that featured an "unsuspecting" menstruating actor at the local mall provoked a fascinating range of responses: only women approached the actor to warn her that she had "leaked," and some approached the actor's *friend* and expressed anger that her friend did not tell her about her stain. At one point, an entire group of teenage boys heckled the actor, laughing and snickering in disgust. As a measure of public attitudes about menstruation, the combination of horror, disgust, pity, and outrage the actor faced testifies directly to the moral panics of menstruation.

Inciting a Moral Panic

> Assuming power is not a straightforward task of taking power
> from one place, transferring it intact, and then and there making
> it one's own; the act of appropriation may involve an alteration
> of power such that the power assumed or appropriated works
> against the power that made that assumption possible. . . .
> in fact, the power assumed may at once retain and resist that
> subordination.
>
> —Judith Butler, *The Psychic Life of Power*

One of the most intriguing (and confusing) aspects of activism—
something the students experienced acutely during this menstrual
activism assignment—is that activists can never fully assess the impact
of their actions on the targeted problem. The students and I both
intended this assignment as a relatively benign intervention that would
introduce students to activism and encourage them to move beyond
merely studying cultural and societal problems by instead prioritizing
interventions. At the completion of the project, I felt proud of the
group, eager to have them present their work at the Moral Panics of
Sexuality conference the following week, and more convinced than
ever that experiential learning has value for feminist education. They
had finished the assignment, I had graded it, and we certainly never
collectively anticipated the social backlash that would soon target these
students' work.

In retrospect, the events that ensued following the menstrual
activism project—our conference losing all state funding, threats of
cancelling our conference, panics about disciplinary action that could
be taken against me or my students, confusion about the difference
between menstruation and masturbation, conflicts between liberals
and conservatives—should not have surprised me as much as they
did. (Social movement scholars suggest that successful progressive
activism often generates conservative countermovements.) After all,
menstruation is a prime target for panicking. The students encountered this even in the most straightforward of activist interventions. In
an all-too-poignant moment of making the Moral Panics of Sexuality
conference *real,* these students had incited a moral panic at precisely
the same time that they would join a group of scholars trying to

understand, deconstruct, and challenge the power of moral panics. We had, in essence, created a moral panic *about* moral panics!

Apparently, the group who had held the signs about menstrual sex ("Honk if you like sex during menstruation!") had, on the day they stood on the corner of campus, been spotted by a staff member of Arizona state representative Linda Gray (R). This staff member, eager to criticize the university for its left-leaning politics, had called Representative Gray to inform her that students held signs "advertising masturbation" on the street corner (somehow *menstruation* and *masturbation* got mixed up). Gray then called the office of the president and provost of the university and demanded the removal of state funding for the conference, citing that female students had worn "lewd" outfits to advertise the conference and that they had openly advertised masturbation on the street. The conference organizers then received an urgent phone call from another university official, asking one of the performance artists to sign a statement that she would not use nudity in her performance and notifying us that these students had engaged in "inappropriate" behavior. All state funding was removed, and, despite having three keynotes booked and a panel of over thirty papers ready to go, the conference organizers questioned whether they might also cancel the conference entirely.

The fact that the group of students whom the elected official had singled out wore jeans and t-shirts, and that the group included a male student, and that they had discussed *menstruation* instead of *masturbation*, that the intervention had nothing to do with advertising the conference had gotten lost amid the collective panicking. As the domino effect of panics unfolded, the staff member passerby panicked. The Republican congresswoman panicked and saw an opportunity to punish a left-leaning university. The media director of the university panicked while fearing bad publicity and reprimand from the president's office. The president and provost panicked, fearing that bad publicity could hurt the funding of the university. The dean panicked, even when expressing political solidarity with the conference. We as conference organizers panicked. Students panicked. The entire scene—straight out of the very core of what our conference had sought to criticize—had unfolded mere days before the conference began.

Nevertheless, the conference unfolded amid the panics with a plethora of panels that showcased the topic as important, complex, and diverse. Several university administrators talked at the conference, showing support as allies with the ideas presented. Students master-fully presented their work, carrying a deep awareness of the potential impact of their seemingly simple interventions. The collective presence of serious work on moral panics managed to counter the panicking in a significant and memorable way—perhaps signaling a bigger lesson about the necessity of meeting moral panics head-on and with the full force of scholarly analysis at hand.

Few pedagogical moments have taught me, or the students, more about the power of simple activist interventions about the body. I had originally learned this when I had assigned a small group of students an extra credit assignment that asked them to grow their body hair for ten weeks and write about it. The results were staggering, repeated again and again over the next five years: students encountered their own, and others', homophobia and heterosexism; they questioned their agency and choice about the body; they confronted their internalized fears of being dirty and unclean; they encountered resistance when they rebelled in the smallest of ways against body norms and "tradi-tional femininity"; and they reported profound changes in conscious-ness about feminism, the body, and the nature of resistance (Fahs 2011a; Fahs 2012a; Fahs and Delgado 2011).

The results for a simple assignment about menstruation seemed equally intense—a sort of "cousin" of the body hair assignment—as the project inspired not only critical thinking about menstruation but also about *moral panics* themselves. Never have I seen students present in a more polished and professional way at a conference, giving voice to their tactical interventions and calling out the audience on any neg-ative menstrual attitudes they harbored. At the conference, one of the presenters, Lorianne Shepard, announced during her talk that she was *currently* menstruating, inspiring much discussion throughout the day about these actions as *brave* and *inspiring*. (Even the mere *mention* of menstruation can set off a firestorm of conversation.) The activist work these students undertook created not only consciousness-raising in the classroom, but it also provoked deep thinking about the narratives of disgust, shame, and hostility that circulate around the menstruating body. Male students, who overwhelmingly committed themselves to the assignment, faced accusations that devalued their manhood. The female students, eager to "out" menstruation in the public sphere, questioned their own feelings about their bodies and asserted them-selves on a seemingly small stage—the campus and community—only to find that they had entered a much larger game—the political battles of the state of Arizona.

As a contribution to the larger conversations about menstrual activism, these activist interventions—and the unexpected consequences of the assignment—suggest that activism must have a place within feminist education. Further, menstrual activism must move beyond its usual target of increasing awareness about the dangers of conventional menstrual products (and the viability of alternative menstrual products like sponges, cups, and make-your-own menstrual pads) by also challenging the *moral panics* of menstruation. It is a particular kind of body—gendered as *female* and *bloody*—that carries the weight of moral panics. The "direct action" tenor of activist work about the body can have significant consequences even for seemingly small and benign interventions. For example, challenging men's attitudes about menstruation and menstrual products, confronting people's resistance to menstrual sex as "dirty" or "disgusting," rebelling against the culture of secrecy and shame around menstruation, expanding the notion of *who menstruates* (via inclusion of trans men and nonmenstruating women), fighting against both consumerism and the pharmaceutical industry, and adopting radical postures of "outing" oneself as menstruating women all symbolize viable strategies of social change for new generations of menstrual activists. By undermining, inciting, interrogating, and dismantling the processes of "menstrual panics"—within or outside of the classroom—menstrual activists can transform small personal rebellions into a forceful call for social justice.

Smear It on Your Face

Menstrual Art, Performance, and Zines as Menstrual Activism

Introduction

For the past four years, I have taught to students in my radical writings and manifestos course a provocative essay by Shannon Docherty (2010) entitled "Smear it on your face, rub it on your body, it's time to start a menstrual party!" Designed as a romp through menarchy—that is, the fusion between menstruation and anarchy—Docherty challenges readers to imagine a new kind of menstrual future, one in which women no longer stay, in Iris Marion Young's (1997) words, "in the menstrual closet" (111). Drawing from this imagined space of leaving the menstrual closet, my final essay in this collection returns to the notion of the menstrual party—a space of joyous, uninhibited, creative menstrual imagination—to outline a future vision for menarchy, including new spaces for menstrual activists to invade and disrupt, new projects to undertake, and reimagined ways to move menstruation out of the closet. Specifically, I examine menstrual art, public menstrual stunts and performance pieces, and menstrual zines, variously imagined, to demonstrate the expansive potential for menstruation to serve as a radical form of feminist resistance.

I take up Chris Bobel's (2006, 2010) claim that menstrual activism might function as the bridge between second- and third-wave feminisms' attitudes toward embodiment, thus exemplifying the best of feminist resistances from multiple generations of scholars and activists. By situating menstruation as both performative fantasy (e.g., blurring the lines between real and fake menstrual blood) and hyperreality (e.g., dealing with the tangible, visceral, potentially abject qualities of menstrual blood, or helping people to become more comfortable with inserting a menstrual cup), this essay critically interrogates what I see as some of the most exciting recent menarchist work and ultimately envisions the future possibilities of menarchy.

In order to think playfully about a menstrual future, or even to understand the potential link between menstruation and political/social resistance, the role of menstrual activism in outlining a vision for "doing feminism" in the third wave warrants consideration. In Judith Lorber's foreword to Chris Bobel's *New Blood* (2010)—notably the only book currently in print about menstrual activism—Lorber writes of the significance of menstrual activism to this particular cultural moment:

> So, in the end, what is the significance of menstrual activism to feminism? The feminist spiritualists join embodiment theory and practice in embracing women's menstruating bodies as beautiful and powerful. The radical genderqueers join feminist postmodernism in challenging the conventional binaries. Using "menstruators" in the narrower sense of people whose bodies bleed periodically rather than equating menstruation with womanhood goes along with the project of detaching sex (body, physiology) from gender (social identity and social status). The anticonsumerists and environmentalists in menstrual activism strengthen like-minded feminists active in other issue-oriented movements—animal rights, veganism, and antiglobalization, for example. Menstrual activism is thus very much part of the feminist third wave—inclusive, conflicted, and contradictory. (xiii–xiv)

Bobel (2010) has in essence outlined not only some of the fascinating contradictions and tensions within menstrual activism (e.g., how do we meaningfully theorize about menstruation without only theorizing about those identified as women? Can we queer menstruation, or does that necessarily strip it of its claims to women as a class?), but she has captured a little known history of people (e.g., the Blood Sisters) working on behalf of undoing and upending traditional menstrual narratives. Her work invites us to ask more expansive questions about menarchy and menstrual activism: What would "in your face" menstrual activism entail? How could it move through and between social spaces? Where does it exist online, or in public, in print, or within/outside the university? Can we envision a communal space to engage menstruation as a social and political force or as something inherently powerful? Can we, in short, actually have a *menstrual party*?

Menstrual Art

Playing with and drawing from the abject qualities of menstrual blood, feminist artists have used menstrual blood to confront sexism and to push the art world's (and art audiences') comfort with women's leaky bodies. For many artists, the presence of menstrual blood has become an *inherently* confrontational device within their work. To expose the workings of the "explicit body," defined as "the explosive literality at the heart of much feminist performance art and performative actions" (Wark 2006, 165), menstrual art has radically upended ideas about menstruation as inherently secretive, hidden, private, feminine, passive, and disgusting. Perhaps more than other forms of art aimed at deconstructing notions of embodiment, menstrual art uniquely attacks and challenges notions of the abject or the "dirty." As Mary Douglas (2002) suggested, the body reveals the boundaries of a culture and "the ordering of a social hierarchy" (7). Menstrual art, then, teeters on the edge of inducing outright panic and introducing chaos into such social hierarchies. As Lisa Tickner (1987) wrote, menstruation *invited* feminist artists to violate the taboo.

In 1973, Mako Idemitsu, a Japanese artist living in the United States, created a video called *What a Woman Made*. The piece featured a blurry image of a tampon slowly oozing blood into a white toilet bowl; over this image, a male voice reads excerpts from the Japanese bestseller *How to Raise Girl Children*. As Jayne Wark (2006) wrote about this piece:

> This misogynistic text barely conceals a revulsion that conflates physiology and personality in an utterly degrading

assessment of the innate nature of Japanese women. They
are described as pieces of property to be safeguarded until
marriage, as lacking talent, and as indecisive and unable
to solve problems by themselves. . . . By thus layering this
aesthetic image with a text that codifies the litany of defects
and negative characteristics imputed to female "nature,"
Idemitsu reveals the impossibility of simply detaching and
reclaiming a "positive" female biological imperative from
the cultural prescriptions that determine and constrain its
meanings. (170)

Idemitsu's work suggests that women cannot merely celebrate menstruation as good, affirming, and joyous; instead, they must use menstrual
blood to directly confront sexist assumptions about women's bodies
and their "inferior" and "dirty" nature.

As another piece that united images and discourses of menstruation with critiques of misogyny and patriarchy, Judy Chicago's
(1972) *The Menstruation Bathroom*, a collaborative project with artist
Miriam Schapiro for *Womanhouse*, featured a bathroom that over-
flowed with menstrual products, featuring boxes filled with new pads
and tampons on the shelves and a trash can filled with bloody pads
featured nearby on the ground. Forcing viewers to confront the abject,
bloody, discarded pads served as a way to imagine both the specific
domestic burdens of managing one's own and others' bodies and the
specific expectations for women to contain their periods effectively and
privately. She predated this piece with *Red Flag* (1971), a lithograph
of a woman pulling a bloody tampon from between her legs, again
inviting viewers to gauge their actual comfort with explicit depictions of menstrual reality. (One can imagine, for example, a vastly
different reaction from those who menstruate and those who do not
menstruate.) This confrontational work refuses to sanitize or contain
the menstrual experience.

Menstrual art has also toyed with the fusion between physical
revulsion, visceral disgust, and menstrual blood. For example, Germaine Greer (1970) dared women to taste their menstrual blood, saying, "If you think you are emancipated, you might consider the idea
of tasting your menstrual blood—if it makes you sick, you've got a
long way to go baby" (Docherty 2010, 2). Building upon this, British
artist Ingrid Berthon-Moine designed for the 2009 Venice Biennale

a piece where she twanged her tampon string to the song "Slave to the Rhythm"; she followed up this piece with a series of twelve photographs that featured women wearing menstrual blood on their lips as a sort of menstrual lipstick (complete with the names of cosmetic colors of red like "Action Red") (Allen 2011; Cochrane 2009). These pieces again play on Kristeva's notion of the abject by bringing menstruation out into the open (in the case of playing the tampon like a guitar) and by bringing it from the vagina to the mouth, inviting audiences to feel "grossed out." Menstruation is "coming out," going public, causing trouble.

Since the second wave of feminism, menstrual artists have continued to provoke and challenge the boundaries of "acceptable" and "respectable" art, figuring women's leaky bodies centrally in this quest. Carlota Berard designed *Aqua Permanens* (2004) where she danced over a piece of cloth and allowed her menstrual blood to drip onto the cloth. Nikoline Calcaterra created *Padded* (year unknown) in honor of Gloria Steinem's "If Men Could Menstruate"; the piece featured a man's vest made solely of tampons, with tampon strings hanging off of the bottom as fringe. Jacquelyn Rixon made *Encrusted Lace* (2009) featuring menstrual blood and glass beads on antique lace and showcasing the visceral qualities of blood-staining. In these three pieces and in nearly all menstrual art, the line between art and activism becomes especially blurry. Operating between the oppressive and the celebratory, the public and the private, the serious and the playful, the shameful and the defiant, menstrual art defies "sanitary" notions of embodiment and instead favors explosive, controversial, and complicated discourses of the body-as-social-text.

Menstrual Stunts

I stain myself, and it does not disgust me. I stain myself, and am not disgusted by myself. I do not reject my body. This is my nature.

—Sangre Menstrual, *Manifesto por la visibilidad de la regla*

Much in line with the tradition of feminist performance art, the notion of public menstrual stunts or performance pieces—designed to confront people's resistances to seeing menstrual blood as visible, real, and tangible, and aiming to reduce the shame and secrecy surrounding menstruation—have offered a provocative and thought-provoking look at the future of menstrual activism. Notably, menstrual activist stunts are certainly not limited geographically or ideologically to the United States; such performances have appeared throughout different parts of Europe as well. Recently, the Spanish performance art group Sangre Menstrual (literally translating to "menstrual blood") staged a series of performances where they engaged in public menstrual stunts throughout the streets of Madrid (Ruddick-Sunstein 2014). In one such stunt, a group of women issued a manifesto entitled *Manifesto for the Visibility of the Period* (2010) and then took to the streets wearing white pants and shorts blatantly stained with menstrual blood. Defiantly joyous and visibly laughing, the group of women walked hand in hand through the streets posting their manifesto and bleeding openly. As *Bust* magazine's Emma Tilden (2014) reported, "Sangre Menstrual wrote the manifesto to point out that, by attempting to hide our periods, a perfectly natural bodily function, we are participating in the patriarchal system and effectively punishing ourselves for being women."

Sangre Menstrual also engaged in a variety of other stunts that coincided with their stained-white-pants performance. In a hybrid between feminist performance art and outright graffiti, the group plastered the streets with photos of shower drains stained with menstrual blood. They also enacted several other activities that sought to make menstruation public: they left globs of menstrual blood on the rim of public trash cans, drew graffiti of menstruating women on city walls, put fake menstrual blood in condoms, wore bloody tampon earrings, painted menstrual hearts on paper and attached them to chain-link fences, put bloodstained fingerprints and handprints on public signs, posted stickers about menstruation on people's backs, distributed copies of their menstruation manifesto, and left scattered bloodstains on public sidewalks. Such performances collectively challenge and extend the notion of graffiti by making public the seemingly invisible, forgotten, or abject qualities of women's leaky bodies.

Norman Mailer (1974) wrote of the political power of graffiti: "For now your name is over their name, over the subway manufacturer, the Transit Authority, the city administration. Your presence is on their presence, your alias hangs over their scene. There is a pleasurable sense of depth in the elusiveness of meaning." The performance by Sangre Menstrual raises questions about the political, social, and even public health significance of using menstrual blood (real or fake, though each has different implications) as "graffiti" that publicly confronts people's disgust about women's bodies and menstrual cycles. For example, in the public comments sections of several online pieces that discussed Sangre Menstrual's work, some readers likened these actions to men wearing semen-soaked pants or spreading semen around publicly on the streets via used condoms. Some equated these performative menstrual blood stunts to the exposure of other sorts of bodily fluids and products like feces and urine. Still others worried about the relationship between menstrual blood and performance art in an age where risks associated with HIV/AIDS remain omnipresent.

The provocations offered by Sangre Menstrual raise questions about why their "graffiti" inspires particular panics at this particular cultural moment, especially as themes of gender violations and disease loom large. Their presence—the presence of menstruating women, and more specifically, of menstruating women with stained pants, bloody hands, and dripping clotty menstrual tissue falling to the ground—on our presence (e.g., the state, the notion of public hygiene or cleanliness, the typical ways that bodies circulate, notions of trash or abjectness, etc.) inspires such panic. Thus, menstrual graffiti may serve as one provocative intervention to make visible the relative invisibility of menstruating women.

Menstrual Zines

I'm just trying to chronicle the number of clues a woman might see each day that say "You are a biohazard."

—Chella Quint, menstrual activist, *Adventures in Menstruating*

Just as menstrual activism serves as a bridge between second- and third-wave feminisms, the menstrual zine—that is, self-produced magazines that exist outside of formal publishing houses and are deeply connected to third-wave feminism (Freedman 2009; Guzzetti and Gamboa 2004)—provides connective tissue between 1990s alt-punk, do-it-yourself culture, and contemporary modes of instant information transmission. Looking at five menstrual zines that I purchased at Left Bank Books in Seattle, Washington, in 2011—Chella Quint's (2009) *Adventures in Menstruating #5*, Cathy Leamy's (2009) *Green Blooded: An Introduction to Eco-Friendly Feminine Hygiene*, Alyssa Beers's (2010) *Menstruation Sensation*, Chella Quint's (2005) *Chart Your Cycle*, and Confluence Media Collective's (2010) *Cuntastic #2: The Menstruation Issue*—the playfulness and subversiveness of the menstrual countercul-ture is clearly visible. Menstrual zines challenge notions of traditional publication venues about women's health (particularly in their rejec-tion of mainstream women's magazines) while also providing a clear subtextual framework for prioritizing women's health and promoting positive and affirming attitudes about menstruation. Written for and by young women, the zines feature a tone of confidence, style, humor, and sarcasm while also giving remarkably accurate information about women's health. If joy can be found in menstruating, the menstrual zine clearly reverberates and resonates with it.

While these five zines took different approaches to critiquing and challenging the mainstream menstrual product industry, with some advocating direct confrontational tactics and others arguing that one should simply abstain from using any disposable products, the dangers of tampons and disposable pads lurked everywhere in these zines. Fighting back against the commercialization of women's bodies and the implied necessity of buying disposable tampons and pads (aka FemCare), each of these zines promoted a range of reus-able products complete with instructions on how to use them, where to obtain them, and why they mattered. *Menstruation Sensation* gave pros and cons for sea sponges, reusable pads, and cups, as did *Chart Your Cycle*, which emphasized how to make your own pads and why charting your cycle can help you avoid (or invite) pregnancy. *Cun-tastic #2* featured an article entitled "The Evils of Disposable Men-strual Products," alongside a clear exposé about mainstream products and their health risks, environmental impact, and possible alternatives to avoid them. Menstrual zines provided in abundance a variety of feminist messages: become responsible about your menstrual habits, stop buying expensive and wasteful products, protect your physi-cal health, and join collective efforts to prioritize women's right to their bodies.

More interestingly, the zines directly and shamelessly confronted ideas about the menstruating body as abject. *Cuntastic #2* featured an explicit piece on menstrual sex called "Earning Your Red Wings," in which the male author Eric Niederkruger describes having sex with a menstruating woman (a fact he discovered only after the lights came on). *Menstruation Sensation* included a section called "Bustin' myths," where the authors address women's fears that reusable products will smell: "Reusable products are still less smelly on the whole than their disposable counterparts. How is this, you may ask? First of all, reusables never sit in the trash (if you have a dog you may very well know the importance of this fact). The cup is made of non-porous material, so it is unable to absorb any smell in the first place. Sea sponges are to be cleaned after each removal. . . . Reusable pads are the same—if changed in an appropriate length of time and soaked and washed well, smell is not an issue either!" *Green Blooded* similarly addressed women's fears about products smelling by writing frankly about the various disadvantages of reusable products. On reusable menstrual pads, the zine notes, "They can get a little stinky if you don't swap them often or if you don't wash them soon after use . . . especially if you forget one for a while." On menstrual cups, the zine says, "If you thought pads and tampons were hands-on. . . . Oh man, cups require intimate handling of your ladyparts, which can be quite a handful for some women." (This latter quote was accompanied by a cartoon that said, "Oops, I 'Pollocked' up the stall again.")

Menstrual zines also did not shy away from recognizing women's periods as difficult, inconvenient, and, at times, downright painful. *Chart Your Cycle* included a list of "Natural options to alleviate cramping," citing exercise, not using tampons, eating vegetables, avoiding caffeine, using cayenne pepper, eliminating aspartame, getting a massage, breathing deeply, and having an orgasm as possible options to lessen pain. The zines also recognized the social difficulties of trying to promote affirmative discourses of menstruation; *Cuntastic #2* included an article called "Mothering a Newly Menstruating Girl" by Heather Hill that detailed the difficulties of teaching her daughter about periods, alongside Jessica Marie's piece, "Giving My Period a New Identity," about making peace with her previously held negative period attitudes. This dual recognition of menstruation as (at times) frustrating but also rewarding charts unique territory for menstrual activists; they simultaneously recognize menstruation as difficult and yet vehemently oppose the elimination of periods, or the shaming of women's bodies, as possible solutions.

Ultimately, menstrual zines advocate a precise emotional tenor that the cultural milieu of menstruation rarely offers elsewhere. It is, at once, rebellious, playful, honest, down-to-earth, smart, savvy, friendly, irreverent, and utilitarian. *Adventures in Menstruating*, for example, featured a section called "Modern Ads Smackdown" where Chella Quint critically tackles a Tampax video, an Always video, and Procter & Gamble's ThermaCare heating pad with humor and wit. She also promotes wearable felt-material menstrual stains (funny, strange, and rebellious), bizarre cartoons of menstrual mishaps, a story by activist-writer Michelle Tea about her friend's tampon sliding out in front of a group of men, and a bullet-pointed guide to having pleasurable menstrual sex. Menstrual zines offer advice, yes, but they also offer an alternative reality. In their world, menstruation is factual and straight-forward but also a source of inspiration, a practical entity worth managing on one's own terms, and something that can start conversations about feminist interventions about the body.

Menstrual Party (Remix)

This is the juice of my bowels, from which I do not run, a limitless stain, a leak that you cannot stop.

—Sangre Menstrual, *Manifesto por la visibilidad de la regla*

I have never been a fan of utopian thinking. As a radical feminist women's studies professor and sex therapist, I care too much about the nuances and imbalances of power to imagine a menstrual utopia of happy bleeding women communing around their bodies and cycles. And yet, everywhere one can feel the currents and tides shifting, moving, demanding a reconsideration of the very nature of what it means to—as the frat boy joke goes—bleed and not die. *Bleed and not die.* Chris Bobel (2010) has argued that menstrual activism stands at the front lines of our feminist future, bridging the gaps in the waves of feminism, and encouraging, radically, a communal consideration of menstruation from women, men, trans folk, environmentalists, genderqueers, academics, activists, feminists, scientists, artists, zine writers, punks, and rebels. Menstruation breaks down barriers between people and ignites a spark of resistance that is both wholly personal and wildly collective. Menstruation invites us to break the taboos—the taboos of sexism and silence and shame and disembodiment; the taboos that menstruation is miserable and lonely; the taboos that enforce a reality where women learn nothing and gain nothing from it, where they don't have any damn fun. In the background of this book, I keep hearing the menstrual activist chant: *Smear it on your face, rub it on your body, it's time to have a menstrual party. It's time to have a menstrual party.* Or Sangre Menstrual: *My flesh is ruled by me. My period is mine.*

These rebellious impulses have particular salience for me in part because I have come to expect the trivialization of my academic subjects and modes of inquiry. Using a radical feminist lens, I write about menstruation, orgasms, body hair, and fatness. I write about emotions, pleasure, relationships, addictions, and forgotten feminist heroes. I am told by some that these are trivial subjects and I should focus on "more important matters." And yet, the moment I hear that these topics are trivial I also learn that menstruation inspires so much panic and distress that my academic conferences are nearly shut down (see chapter 10) and I am called, by Ann Coulter's friends, a Communist and a revolutionary for merely writing about it. Everywhere I see, hear, and feel the tremors of women getting angrier and more defiant about the suppression of their physical and bodily realities; everywhere I sense an impulse to *bleed and not die*, to cackle while doing so.

The body, after all, absorbs, reflects, and mirrors the fundamental social forces of our times. In every accusation of the trivial, there lurks recognition of power, validation for the potential for resistance, celebration of the inherently radical nature of women using their bodies and their words to resist the limited narratives they have so long believed to be true and inevitable. Women in the United States and throughout the world have become embattled in a fight for basic human dignity and rights to their bodies. Abortion. Rape. Female Genital Cutting. Plastic Surgery. Childbirth. Minimum Wage. Sexual Autonomy. Birth Control. Worker's Compensation. Immigration. Representation. These subjects, however degraded and distorted by popular media and news sites, reveal much about the serious and nontrivial intrusions and degradations women face on a near-daily basis.

At its core, this book shows how the menstruating body presents a threat to the existing social order, yielding new and productive spaces to imagine different menstrual futures. Menstruation disrupts the boundaries of patriarchy, underscores the realities of misogyny, and teases apart the tensions between feminists and their allies and enemies. I hear laughter at the margins of these menstrual conversations, a playful defiance at the suggestion of continued menstrual silence. Like our cycles, I imagine menstrual resistance coming forth in waves, sometimes slowly—drip, drip, drip—and sometimes gushing forcefully outward, making a mess, leaving stains. The impulse to write a new story, to resist, to fight back, to destroy conventional narratives of our bodies and sexualities is there, waiting on the margins, impatient, feral. We are out for blood, ready to use our menstruating bodies as weapons, as tools, as markers of the absurd, as performative utterances, as devices of wild and persistent optimism. We are out for blood.

Acknowledgments

All aspects of my life, especially my intellectual life, have been made richer and fuller by the study of the body and its attendant intensities, knowledges, and resonances. That I have arrived now at the study of menstruation is a consequence of that wondrous mix of good luck and excellent mentoring. In quite the happenstance manner, I had been perusing the latest calls for papers in various feminist journals and found one that asked for papers about blood. I had just finished a study about women's sexuality and had some data on women's attitudes about having sex during menstruation; consequently, I began writing a piece about menstrual sex and published it in *Feminism & Psychology* a few years later. Without the warm encouragement of Virginia Braun, editor at *F&P*, and Joan Chrisler, who attended a talk I gave about that piece at the Association for Women in Psychology back in 2012 and invited me to join the club of menstrual researchers, I may not have pursued work on menstruation much further. I am forever in their debt for pushing me to continue to examine menstruation as a fruitful site for deep and meaningful work about sexism, oppression, bodies, intersectionality, and, of course, feminist resistance.

I feel enormous, unending gratitude to the group of scholar-activists I affectionately call the "menstrual mafia"—women (and one man) who have organized and run the Society for Menstrual Cycle Research for years and who have collectively created and sustained my single favorite feminist organization and feminist conference on earth. These scholars include: Chris Bobel, Joan Chrisler, Ingrid Johnston-Robledo, Elizabeth Kissling, Maureen McHugh, David Linton, Mindy Erchull, Heather Dillaway, Laura Wershler, Evelina Sterling, Jerilynn Prior, Tomi-Ann Roberts, Peggy Stubbs, Jennifer Gorman,

Chris Hitchcock, Lisa Leger, Sheryl Mendlinger, Janette Perz, and Jane Ussher. Every two years we convene to talk about menstruation, embodiment, activism, public health, reproduction, and rebellion; I look forward with gusto to each and every encounter I have with them. If anyone can bridge the gap between "sisterhood is powerful" and contemporary debates about feminism (What is a woman? Third-wave contributions to feminism?), this group absolutely can. Thank you thank you thank you.

I owe a sizeable debt to Chris Bobel, whose work on menstrual activism (*New Blood*) and whose spirited encouragement exemplifies the best of what we do (or hope to do). You. Are. Amazing. Rebecca Plante and Andrew Smiler, writing group friends extraordinaire, you played a major role in helping me to think through the design of this book, its importance, and how to defy my own fears and anxieties about the blank page; you two keep me working and laughing in equal measure. Carla Golden, thanks for reminding me why writing (inexpensive) books matters and why having undergrads read them is the highest of honors. Thanks to my dear friend, Mary Dudy, for translating the *Manifesto for the Visibility of Menstruation*—and for the funniest damn emails on the planet sent from the wilds of Cambridge and beyond. Sara McClelland, for your honest talk of blood and bodies, and for your eerily intuitive sense of knowing what to say (and exactly when to say it), I adore you forever and ever.

I feel intense gratitude and awe toward the menstrual activists and artists I have had the privilege to know in these past several years. Diana Álvarez, goddess of all things bloody, your work is so far on the edge that it blows my mind. Sadie Mohler, who manages radiance and radicalism in equal measure, thank you for your soulful art and sisterly love. Echo Thunderbolt, your beautifully witchy vision of the world—how it is, how it could be—keeps me questioning and is forever inspiring—I'll come find you in the forest one of these days. Chella Quint, staining the world with your brilliance, keep on keeping on.

Without my students, especially those in the Feminist Research on Gender and Sexuality Group, this book would not exist. They continue to put menstruation on the map and have undertaken brave and important work that delights and inspires me. Special thanks to Kimberly Koerth, who read and edited every word of this book several times over, for your brilliance, crazy humor, and goodwill. Thanks to the FROGS: Natali Blazevic, Michael Karger, Adrielle Munger, Jax

Gonzalez, Stephanie Robinson-Cestaro, Rose Coursey, Crystal Zaragoza (who translated many a document!), Laura Martinez, Chelsea Pixler Charbonneau, Kimberly Koerth, Corie Cisco, Elizabeth Wallace, Marissa Loiacono, and Eva Sisko, and to all the students I worked with on menstrual activism over the years. The boundless enthusiasm and energy they direct toward this topic—and their uncommon generosity, intelligence, kindness, and humor—have literally transformed the conditions in which I work and have motivated me to be braver and more persistent than I ever thought possible.

Thanks to my colleagues and comrades near and far, many of whom have traveled with me on this journey of academic life for a decade or more. Special thanks to Marlene Tromp, Louis Mendoza, Sharon Kirsch, Michael Stancliff, Monica Casper, Patrick Grzanka, Rosalind Gill, Lauren Griswold, Michelle Tellez, Rose Carlson, Michelle Tea, Valerie Kemper, Deborah Tolman, Ela Przybylo, Bernadette Barton, Leonore Tiefer, and Virginia Braun. I am grateful for the financial support provided by the Center for Critical Inquiry and Cultural Studies, the Institute for Humanities Research, and the School for Humanities, Arts, and Cultural Studies as I finished the book. Thanks to Adrian Rogers for indexing the book so thoroughly. Thanks also to Amy Scholder, Larin McLaughlin, and Felicity Plester, for publishing my previous books with such energy, care, and thoughtfulness, and to Beth Bouloukos, Laurie Searl, Dana Foote, and SUNY Press, for believing in this book and seeing it through.

I owe this book and so much more to my feminist mothers and mentors, all of whom have inspired and protected me, and, in the process, grown me up. Deb Martinson, who died of breast cancer in April 2014, I miss your joyful, spunky, ferociously funny self every damn day—thank you for loving me and the work so much. Sarah Stage, my wicked historian mentor and wonderful friend, who insists on delectable prosecco and fancy cheese, thank you for your steady and generous ways. Abby Stewart, who nudged me in the right direction, paved the way, and invested so much into me, I am forever in your debt. Jane Caputi, who makes radical feminism look like the best possible party, and who tells stories like no other, I adore you. Ti-Grace Atkinson, there will never be words for how much our friendship has meant to me, nor for how much you mean to the world. Roxanne Dunbar-Ortiz, Dana Densmore, Carol Giardina, and Kathie Sarachild, you've bled for us all.

The richness of my friendships, and the echoes of our many conversations and years together, sustain my spirit and underlie the joy I take in writing each book. Elmer Griffin, for teaching me to keep a steady hand, I carry you with me now and always. Lori Errico-Seaman, Sean Seaman, Sara McClelland, Mary Dudy, Jennifer Tamir, Denise Delgado, Garyn Tsuru, Annika Mann, Jan Habarth, Marcy Winokur, Steve DuBois, Kelly Rafferty, Wendy D'Andrea, Connie Hardesty, and David Frost, I love you all. To Eric Swank, who has always encouraged me to be out for blood, and whom I love in the most intense and feral ways, I know how much you believe in my work (and how much it sometimes costs you) and I will never forget it. To my mother, my roots, my origin, for keeping my feet firmly planted in the earth, thank you. Finally, I dedicate this book to my sister, my blood, Kristen (Fahs) Nusbaum, whom I've bled with for more of my life than anyone else. This book is also for her blood, the gorgeous and effervescent Simon and Ryan, for reminding me just how deep and wild the love of siblings can run.

∼

An earlier version of chapter 1 appeared in *Women's Reproductive Health* (2014) 1(2):90–105 (with Jax Gonzalez, Rose Coursey, and Stephanie Robinson-Cestaro) and the current version appears here with permission of Taylor & Francis. Earlier versions of "Dispatches from the Blogosphere" appeared in *Re:Cycling*, the blog for the Society for Menstrual Cycle Research. Chapter 10 is reproduced with permission of Palgrave Macmillan from *The Moral Panics of Sexuality* (2013), edited by Breanne Fahs, Mary L. Dudy, and Sarah Stage.

References

Acker, Joan. 2006. "Inequality Regimes: Gender, Class, and Race in Organizations." *Gender & Society* 20(4): 441–464.

Adams, Simon, and Raelene Frances. 2003. "Lifting the Veil: The Sex Industry, Museums, and Galleries." *Labour History* 85: 47–64.

Allen, Katherine, and Abbie Goldberg. 2009. "Sexual Activity during Menstruation: A Qualitative Study." *Journal of Sex Research* 46(6): 535–545.

Allen, Polly. 2011. "In the Frame: Ingrid Berthon-Moine: Lipstick and Looking Twice." *Bitch.* http://bitchmagazine.org/post/in-the-frame-ingrid-berthon-moine-lipstick-and-looking-twice.

Arden, Madelynne, Louise Dye, and Anne Walker. 1999. "Menstrual Synchrony: Awareness and Subjective Experiences." *Journal of Reproductive and Infant Psychology* 17(3): 255–265.

Armstrong, Elizabeth A., and Laura T. Hamilton. 2013. *Paying for the Party: How College Maintains Inequality.* Cambridge: Harvard University Press.

Ashmore, Richard, Kay Deaux, and Tracy McLaughlin-Volpe. 2004. "An Organizing Framework for Collective Identity: Articulation and Significance of Multidimensionality." *Psychological Bulletin* 130(1): 80–114.

Atkinson, Ti-Grace. 1974. *Amazon Odyssey.* New York: Links Books.

Bae, Michelle. 2011. "Interrogating Girl Power: Girlhood, Popular Media, and Postfeminism." *Visual Arts Research* 37(2): 28–40.

Berg, D., and L. Block Coutts. 1994. "The Extended Curse: Being a Woman Every Day." *Health Care for Women International* 15(1): 11–22.

Bettie, Julie. 2003. *Women without Class: Girls, Race, and Identity.* Berkeley: University of California Press.

Blood Sisters. 2010. "Hot Pants: Do It Yourself Gynecology." http://www.indybay.org/newsitems/2010/04/06/18643940.php.

Bobel, Chris. 2006. " 'Our Revolution Has Style': Contemporary Menstrual Product Activists 'Doing Feminism' in the Third Wave." *Sex Roles* 54(5–6): 331–345.

Bobel, Chris. 2007. " 'I'm Not an Activist, Though I've Done a Lot of It': Doing Activism, Being Activist, and the 'Perfect Standard' in a Contemporary Movement." *Social Movement Studies* 6(2): 147–159.

Bobel, Chris. 2008. "From Convenience to Hazard: A Short Story of the Emergence of the Menstrual Activism Movement, 1971–1992." *Health Care for Women International* 29(7): 738–754.

Bobel, Chris. 2010. *New Blood: Third Wave Feminism and the Politics of Menstruation.* Camden: Rutgers University Press.

Bodkin, Alison. 2012, Nov 8. "Nursing Our Pinkoberfest Hangover." *In Media Res.* http://mediacommons.futureofthebook.org/imr/2012/11/08/nursing-our-pinktoberfest-hangover.

Brain, James L. 1988. "Male Menstruation in History and Anthropology." *The Journal of Psychohistory* 15(3): 311–323.

Briefel, Aviva. 2005. "Monster Pains: Masochism, Menstruation, and Identification in the Horror Film." *Film Quarterly* 58(3): 16–27.

Bryant, Alyssa N. 2003. "Changes in Attitudes toward Women's Roles: Predicting Gender Role Traditionalism among College Students." *Sex Roles* 28: 131–142.

Bull, J. J., Tim S. Jessop, and Marvin Whiteley. 2010. "Deathly Drool: Evolutionary and Ecological Basis of Septic Bacteria in Komodo Dragon Mouths." *PloS one* 5(6): e11097.

Burley, Nancy. 1979. "The Evolution of Concealed Ovulation." *American Naturalist* 114(6): 835–858.

Butler, Judith. 1997. *The Psychic Life of Power: Theories in Subjection.* Palo Alto: Stanford University Press.

Carpenter, Laurel. 2009. The Menstruation Issue (#2). *Cuntastic: A Journal of Sexual & Reproductive Freedom.* http://blog.cuntastic.org/zine/.

Case, Charles E., and Cameron D. Lippard. 2009. "Humorous Assaults on Patriarchal Ideology." *Sociological Inquiry* 79(2): 240–255.

Chesler, Phyllis. 2005. *Women and Madness.* New York: Palgrave Macmillan.

Chrisler, Joan. 2008. "PMS as a Culture-Bound Syndrome." In *Lectures on the Psychology of Women*, 4th edition, edited by Joan Chrisler, Carla Golden, and Patricia D. Rozee, 155–171. New York: McGraw-Hill.

Chrisler, Joan C. 1996. "PMS as a Culture-Bound Syndrome." In *Lectures on the Psychology of Women*, edited by Joan C. Chrisler, Carla Golden, and Patricia D. Rozee, 106–121. New York: McGraw-Hill.

Chrisler, Joan C. 2011. "Leaks, Lumps, and Lines: Stigma and Women's Bodies." *Psychology of Women Quarterly* 35: 202–214.

Chrisler, Joan C., Ingrid K. Johnson, Nicole M. Champagna, and Kathleen E. Preston. 1994. "Menstrual Joy: The Construct and Its Consequences." *Psychology of Women Quarterly* 18(3): 375–387.

Christina, Dominique. 2014. "The Period Poem." *Upworthy.* http://www.upworthy.com/if-youre-too-grossed-out-to-share-this-video-then-youre-exactly-why-it-exists.

Ciofi, C. 1999, March. "The Komodo Dragon." *Scientific American.* http://www.google.com/url?sa=t&rct=j&q=&esrc=s&source=web&cd=1&cad=rja&uact=8&ved=0CB4QFjAA&url=http%3A%2F%2Fsiamdivers.

com%2Fdownloads%2FKomodo_Dragons.pdf&ei=62yPVLXwHZflo
ATDvIKICg&usg=AFQjCNHu1JxeY-RC5W-AoIIZ9WRDqFMg8A.

Clancy, Kate. 2011. "Do Women in Groups Bleed Together? On Menstrual Synchrony." *Scientific American Blog.* http://blogs.scientificamerican. com/context-and-variation/2011/11/16/menstrual-synchrony/.

CNN Money. 2012a. "Best Jobs in America." http://money.cnn.com/pf/ best-jobs/2012/.

CNN Money. 2012b. "100 Best Companies to Work For." http://money.cnn. com/magazines/fortune/best-companies/2012/benefits/sabbaticals.html.

Cochrane, Kira. 2009. "It's in the Blood." *The Guardian.* http://www.the-guardian.com/lifeandstyle/2009/oct/02/menstruation-feminist-activists.

Collett, Mabt, Grace Wertenberger, and Virginia Fiske. 1955. "The Menstrual Cycle: The Effect of Age upon the Pattern of the Menstrual Cycle." *Obstetrical & Gynecological Survey* 10(5): 706–707.

Collins, Petra. 2013. "Censorship and the Female Body." *Petra Collins.* http:// www.petracollins.com/?page_id=222.

Copp, Martha, and Sherryl Kleinman. 2008. "Practicing What We Teach: Feminist Strategies for Teaching about Sexism." *Feminist Teacher* 18: 101–124

Cornwall, Andrea. 2007. "Myths to Live By? Female Solidarity and Female Autonomy Reconsidered." *Development & Change* 38(1): 149–168.

Davidson, Anna. 2012. "Narratives of Menstrual Product Consumption: Convenience, Culture, or Commoditization?" *Bulletin of Science, Technology, & Society* 32(1): 56–70.

Daw, Jennifer. 2002. "Is PMDD Real?" *APA Monitor* 33(9): 58.

Dean, Jodi. 1997. "Feminist Solidarity, Reflective Solidarity: Theorizing Connections after Identity Politics." *Women & Politics* 18(4): 1–26.

Delaney, Janice, Mary Lupton, and Emily Toth. 1988. *The Curse: A Cultural History of Menstruation.* Chicago: University of Illinois Press.

Dobrzynski, Judith H. 2011. "Fire in Their Bellies: On the Irresponsibility of All Involved in the 'Hide/Seek' Controversy." *Pundicity.* http://www. judithdobrzynski.com/9519/fire-in-their-bellies.

Docherty, Shannon. 2010. "Smear It on Your Face, Rub It on Your Body, It's Time to Start a Menstrual Party!" *CTSJ: Critical Theory and Social Justice* 1(1). http://scholar.oxy.edu/ctsj/vol1/iss1/12/.

Douglas, Mary. 2002. *Purity and Danger: An Analysis of Concepts of Pollution and Taboo.* London: Routledge & Kegan Paul.

Dunbar, Roxanne. 1974. *Female Liberation as a Basis for Social Revolution.* Boston: New England Free Press.

Dunnavant, Nicki, and Tomi-Ann Roberts. 2013. "Restriction and Renewal, Pollution and Power, Constraint and Community: The Paradoxes of Religious Women's Experiences of Menstruation." *Sex Roles* 68(1–2): 121–131.

Dworkin, Andrea. 1989. *Letters from a War Zone.* New York: Dutton.

Echols, Alice. 1989. *Daring to Be Bad: Radical Feminism in America, 1967–1975*. Minneapolis: University of Minnesota Press.

Edmonds, M. 2010. "Stuff Mom Never Told You about Iconic Cosmetics and Menstrual Synchrony." *How Stuff Works Blog.* http://blogs.how-stuffworks.com/2010/10/08/stuff-mom-never-told-you-about-iconic-cosmetics-and-menstrual-synchrony/.

England, Paula. 2010. "The Gender Revolution: Uneven and Stalled." *Gender & Society* 24(2): 149–166.

Enns, Carolyn Zerbe, and Ada L. Sinacore. 2004. *Teaching and Social Justice: Integrating Multicultural and Feminist Theories in the Classroom.* Washington, DC: American Psychological Association.

Erchull, Mindy J., Joan C. Chrisler, Jennifer A. Gorman, and Ingrid Johnston-Robledo. 2002. "Education and Advertising: A Content Analysis of Commercially Produced Booklets about Menstruation." *Journal of Early Adolescence* 22(4): 455–474.

Fahs, Breanne. 2011a. *Performing Sex: The Making and Unmaking of Women's Erotic Lives.* Albany: State University of New York Press.

Fahs, Breanne. 2011b. "Dreaded 'Otherness': Heteronormative Patrolling in Women's Body Hair Rebellions." *Gender & Society* 25(4): 451–472.

Fahs, Breanne. 2011c. "Sex during Menstruation: Race, Sexual Identity, and Women's Qualitative Accounts of Pleasure and Disgust." *Feminism & Psychology* 21(2): 155–178.

Fahs, Breanne. 2012a. "Breaking Body Hair Boundaries: Classroom Exercises for Challenging Social Constructions of the Body and Sexuality." *Feminism & Psychology* 22(4): 482–506.

Fahs, Breanne. 2012b. "'Feminine Hygiene' and the Ultimate Double Standard." *Re:Cycling.* http://menstruationresearch.org/2012/09/19/feminine-hygiene-and-the-ultimate-double-standard/.

Fahs, Breanne. 2013a. "Raising Bloody Hell: Inciting Menstrual Panics through Campus and Community Activism." In *The Moral Panics of Sexuality*, edited by Breanne Fahs, Mary Dudy, and Sarah Stage, 77–91. London: Palgrave.

Fahs, Breanne. 2013b. "Shaving It All Off: Examining Social Norms of Body Hair among College Men in a Women's Studies Course." *Women's Studies: An Interdisciplinary Journal* 42(5): 559–577.

Fahs, Breanne. 2014. "Perilous Patches and Pitstaches: Imagined versus Lived Experiences of Women's Body Hair Growth." *Psychology of Women Quarterly* 38(2): 167–180.

Fahs, Breanne, and Denise A. Delgado. 2011. "The Specter of Excess: Race, Class, and Gender in Women's Body Hair Narratives." In *Embodied Resistance: Breaking the Rules, Challenging the Norms*, edited by Chris Bobel and Samantha Kwan, 13–25. Nashville: Vanderbilt University Press.

Farber, Barry A. 2003. "Patient Self-Disclosure: A Review of the Research." *Journal of Clinical Psychology* 59(5): 589–600.

Farrer, Claire R. 1980. "Singing for Life: The Mescalero Apache Girl's Puberty Ceremony." In *Betwixt & Between: Patterns of Masculine and Feminine Initiation*, edited by Louise Carus Mahdi, Steven Foster, and Meredith Little, 239–263. Chicago: Open Court.

Feasey, Rebecca. 2006. "Watching Charmed: Why Teen Television Appeals to Women." *Journal of Popular Film & Television* 34(1): 2–9.

Fischer, Agneta H., Antony Manstead, Catharine Evers, Monique Timmers, and Guido Valk. 2004. "Motives and Norms Underlying Emotional Regulation." In *The Regulation of Emotion*, edited by Pierre Philippot and Robert S. Feldman, 187–210. Florence: Psychology Press.

Foucault, Michel. 1983. "Vous êtes dangereux." *Libération*. Reprinted by Didier Eribon (1991). http://1libertaire.free.fr/Foucault36.html.

Fraser, Lin. 2009. "Depth Psychotherapy with Transgender People." *Sexual and Relationship Therapy* 24(2): 126–142.

Freedman, Jenna. 2009. "Grrrl Zines in the Library." *Signs* 35(1): 52–59.

Frisch, Rose. 1984. "Body Fat, Puberty, and Fertility." *Biological Reviews* 59(2): 161–188.

Frost, Stuart. 2008. "Secret Museums: Hidden Histories of Sex and Sexuality." *Museums & Social Issues* 3(1): 29–40.

Frye, Marilyn. 1983. *The Politics of Reality: Essays in Feminist Theory*. Trumansburg: Crossing Press.

Giami, Alain J., and Emmanuelle Beaubatie. 2011. "Transgender Identities and Practices: Preliminary Results of a National Multi-Centric Survey in France." *Journal of Sexual Medicine* 8: 95–96.

Gill, Rosalind. 2007. "Critical Respect: The Difficulties and Dilemmas of Agency and 'Choice' for Feminism." *European Journal of Women's Studies* 14(1): 69–80.

Gillespie, Rosemary. 2003. "Childfree and Feminine: Understanding the Gender Identity of Voluntarily Childless Women." *Gender & Society* 17(1): 122–136.

Goldberg, Michelle. 2014. "What Is a Woman? The Dispute between Radical Feminism and Transgenderism." *The New Yorker*. http://www.newyorker.com/magazine/2014/08/04/woman-2.

Goldman, S., and H. Schneider. 1987. "Menstrual Synchrony: Social and Personality Factors." *Journal of Social Behavior and Personality* 2: 243–250.

Graham, Colin, and William McGrew. 1980. "Menstrual Synchrony in Female Undergraduates Living on a Coeducational Campus." *Psychoneuroendocrinology* 5(3): 245–252.

Greer, Germaine. 1970. *The Female Eunuch*. London: MacGibbon & Kee.

Griffin, R. Morgan. 2012. "Coping with Excess Sleepiness." *Web MD*. http://www.webmd.com/sleep-disorders/excessive-sleepiness-10/shift-work.

Gurin, Patricia, Arthur Miller, and Gerald Gurin. 1980. "Stratum Identification and Consciousness." *Social Psychology Quarterly* 43(1): 30–47.

Guterman, Mark A., Payal Mehta, and Margaret S. Gibbs. 2008. "Menstrual Taboos among Major Religions." *The Internet Journal of World Health and Societal Politics* 5(2). http://ispub.com/IJWH/5/2/8213.

Guzzetti, Barbara J., and Margaret Gamboa. 2004. "Zines for Social Justice: Adolescent Girls Writing on Their Own." *Reading Research Quarterly* 39(4): 408–436.

Harris, Amy, and Virginia Vitzthum. 2013. "Darwin's Legacy: An Evolutionary View of Women's Reproductive and Sexual Functioning." *Journal of Sex Research* 50(3–4): 207–246.

Harris, Karen L., Kari Melaas, and Edyth Rodacker. 1999. "The Impact of Women's Studies Courses on College Students of the 1990s." *Sex Roles* 40: 969–977.

Hartung, Beth. 1990. "Selective Rejection: How Students Perceive Women's Studies Teachers." *NWSA Journal* 2: 254–263.

Heatherington, Laurie, Joseph Stets, and Susan Mazzarella. 1986. "Whither the Bias: The Female Client's 'Edge' in Psychotherapy?" *Psychotherapy: Theory, Research, Practice, Training* 23(2): 252–256.

Hemmings, Clare. 2012. "Affective Solidarity: Feminist Reflexivity and Political Transformation." *Feminist Theory* 13(2): 147–161.

Henderson-King, Donna, and Abigail J. Stewart. 1999. "Educational Experiences and Shifts in Group Consciousness." *Personality and Social Psychology Bulletin* 25: 390–399.

Hess, Amanda. 2010, October 5. "Museum of Menstruation Consumed Maryland Man Harry Finley." *TBD* . . . http://www.tbd.com/blogs/amanda-hess/2010/10/museum-of-menstruation-consumed-maryland-man-harry-finley-2697.html.

Hines, Alice. 2013. "The Rise of the Period Apps: Where Big Data Meets Girlie Graphics." *New York Magazine.* http://nymag.com/the-cut/2013/08/period-apps-where-big-data-meets-girly-graphics.html.

Hinshaw, Stephen P. 2007. *The Mark of Shame: Stigma of Mental Illness and an Agenda for Change.* New York: Oxford University Press.

Huffington Post. 2012. "Night Shift May Raise Men's Prostate Cancer Risk, and 7 Other Ways It Could Impact Health." *Huffington Post Healthy Living.* http://www.huffingtonpost.com/2012/10/25/night-shift-prostate-cancer-health_n_2003392.html.

Israel, Tania, Raia Gorcheva, William A. Walther, Joselyne M. Sulzner, and Jessye Cohen. 2008. "Therapists' Helpful and Unhelpful Situations with LGBT Clients: An Exploratory Study." *Professional Psychology: Research and Practice* 39(3): 361–368.

Itzkoff, Dave. 2010, December 1. "National Portrait Gallery Removes Video Criticized for Religious Imagery." *New York Times Arts Beat.* http://arts-beat.blogs.nytimes.com/2010/12/01/national-portrait-gallery-removes-video-criticized-for-religious-imagery/?scp=2&sq=national%20portrait%20gallery&st=cse&_r=0.

Jackson, Theresa, and Rachel Falmagne. 2013. "Women Wearing White: Discourses of Menstruation and the Experience of Menarche." *Feminism & Psychology* 23(3): 379–398.

Jarett, Laura. 1984. "Psychosocial and Biological Influences on Menstruation: Synchrony, Cycle Length, and Regularity." *Psychoneuroendocrinology* 9(1): 21–28.

Johnston-Robledo, Ingrid, Melissa Ball, Kimberly Lauta, and Ann Zekoll. 2003. "To Bleed or Not to Bleed: Young Women's Attitudes toward Menstrual Suppression." *Women & Health* 38(3): 59–75.

Johnston-Robledo, Ingrid, Jessica Barnack, and Stephanie Wares. 2006. "'Kiss Your Period Goodbye': Menstrual Suppression in the Popular Press." *Sex Roles* 54(5–6): 353–360.

Johnston-Robledo, Ingrid, Kristin Sheffield, Jacqueline Voigt, and Jennifer Wilcox-Constantine. 2007. "Reproductive Shame: Self-Objectification and Young Women's Attitudes toward Their Reproductive Functioning." *Women & Health* 46(1): 25–39.

Johnston-Robledo, Ingrid, and Margaret L. Stubbs. 2013. Positioning Periods: Menstruation in Social Context: An Introduction to a Special Issue. *Sex Roles* 68(1–2):1–8.

Kerkham, Patricia. 2003. "Menstruation—The Gap in the Text?" *Psychoanalytic Psychotherapy* 17(4): 279–299.

Kiltie, Richard. 1982. "On the Significance of Menstrual Synchrony in Closely Associated Women." *American Naturalist* 119(3): 414–419.

King, Samantha. 2006. *Pink Ribbons, Inc.: Breast Cancer and the Politics of Philanthropy.* Minneapolis: University of Minnesota Press.

Kissling, Elizabeth Arveda. 1996a. "Bleeding Out Loud: Communication about Menstruation." *Feminism & Psychology* 6(4): 481–504.

Kissling, Elizabeth. 1996b. "'That's Just a Basic Teen-Age Rule': Girls' Linguistic Strategies for Managing the Menstrual Communication Taboo." *Journal of Applied Communication Research* 24(4): 292–309.

Kissling, Elizabeth A. 2002. "On the Rag on Screen: Menarche in Film and Television." *Sex Roles* 46 (1–2): 5–12.

Kissling, Elizabeth. 2006. *Capitalizing on the Curse: The Business of Menstruation.* Boulder: Lynne Rienner.

Kissling, Elizabeth. 2010. "Body Scans, Disability, Menstruation, and Security Theatre." *Re:Cycling.* http://menstruationresearch.org/2010/01/05/body-scans-disability-menstruation-and-security-theatre/.

Klebanoff, Nina, and Patsy Keyser. 1996. "Menstrual Synchronization: A Qualitative Study." *Journal of Holistic Nursing* 14(2): 98–114.

Knowlton, Nancy. 1979. "Reproductive Synchrony, Parental Investment, and the Evolutionary Dynamics of Sexual Selection." *Animal Behavior* 27(4): 1022–1033.

Knutsson, Anders. 2003. "Health Disorders of Shift Workers." *Occupational Medicine* 53(2): 103–108.

Koedt, Anne, Ellen Levine, and Anita Rapone. 1973. *Radical Feminism*. New York: Quadrangle Books.

Koff, Elissa, and Jill Reirdan. 1995. "Preparing Girls for Menstruation: Recommendations from Adolescent Girls. *Adolescence* 30(120): 795–811.

Koutroulis, Glenda. 2001. "Soiled Identity: Memory-Work Narratives of Menstruation." *Health* 5(2): 187–205.

Kozee, Holly B., Tracy L. Tylka, and L. Andrew Bauerband. 2012. "Measuring Transgender Individuals' Comfort with Gender Identity and Appearance: Development and Validation of the Transgender Congruence Scale." *Psychology of Women Quarterly* 36(2): 179–196.

Kravetz, Diane, Jeanne Marecek, and Stephen Finn. 1983. "Factors Influencing Women's Participation in Consciousness-Raising Groups." *Psychology of Women Quarterly* 7(3): 257–271.

Kristeva, Julia. 1982. *Powers of Horror: An Essay on Abjection*. New York: Columbia University Press.

Lalor, Katie, and Ginger Gorman. 2012, May 23. "Pornography, Sex, and Censorship: Australia's Erotic History." *ABC News*. http://www.abc.net.au/local/stories/2012/05/23/3509073.htm.

Lee, Janet. 1994. "Menarche and the (Hetero)sexualization of the Female Body." *Gender & Society* 8(3): 343–362.

Lee, Shirley. 2002. "Health and Sickness: The Meaning of Menstruation and Premenstrual Syndrome in Women's Lives." *Sex Roles* 46(1–2): 25–35.

Leite, Jorge. 2012. "Transit to Where? Monstrosity, (De)pathologization, Social Insecurity, and Transgender Identities." *Estudos Feministas* 20(2): 559–568.

Levitt, Heidi M., and Maria R. Ippoliti. 2013. "Navigating Minority Stressors and Developing Authentic Self-Presentation." *Psychology of Women Quarterly* 38(1): 46–64.

Liddle, Becky. 1997. "Gay and Lesbian Clients' Selection of Therapists and Utilization of Therapy." *Psychotherapy: Theory, Research, Practice, Training* 34(1): 11–18.

Little, Bertis, David Guzick, Robert Malina, and M. Ferreira. 1989. "Environmental Influences Cause Menstrual Synchrony, Not Pheromones." *American Journal of Human Biology* 1(1): 53–57.

Lloyd, Elisabeth. 2006. *The Case of the Female Orgasm: Bias in the Science of Evolution*. Cambridge: Harvard University Press.

Lorber, Judith. 2010. Foreword. In *New Blood: Third Wave Feminism and the Politics of Menstruation*, by Chris Bobel, xi–xiv. New Brunswick: Rutgers University Press.

Ludlow, John. 1866. *Woman's Work in the Church: Historical Notes on Deaconesses and Sisterhoods*. London: Alexander Strahan.

Lupton, Mary Jane. 1993. *Menstruation & Psychoanalysis*. Chicago: University of Illinois Press.

MacDonald, Eleanor. 1998. "Critical Identities: Rethinking Feminism through Transgender Politics." *Atlantis: A Women's Studies Journal* 23: 3–12.

MacDonald, Shauna M. 2007. "Leaky Performances: The Transformative Potential of Menstrual Leaks." *Women's Studies in Communication* 30(3): 340–357.

MacLeod, Nadia. 2013. "Menstrual Synchrony." http://www.menstruation.com.au/periodpages/menstrualsynchrony.html.

Maher, Frances A. 1999. "Progressive Education and Feminist Pedagogies: Issues in Gender, Power, and Authority." *Teachers College Record* 101(1): 35–59.

Mailer, Norman. 1974, May. "The Faith of Graffiti." *Esquire*. http://testpressing.org/2012/06/esquire-the-faith-of-graffiti-norman-mailer/.

Mansfield, Phyllis K., and Margaret L. Stubbs. 2007. "The Menstrual Cycle: Feminist Research from the Society for Menstrual Cycle Research." *Women & Health* 46(1): 1–5.

Martin, Emily. 2001. *The Woman in the Body: A Cultural Analysis of Reproduction*. Boston: Beacon Press.

Marván, Maria Luisa, Claudia Morales, and Sandra Cortés-Iniestra. 2006. "Emotional Reactions to Menarche among Mexican Women of Different Generations." *Sex Roles* 54(5–6): 323–330.

Matteo, Sherri. 1987. "The Effect of Job Stress and Job Interdependency on Menstrual Cycle Length, Regularity, and Synchrony." *Psychoneuroendocrinology* 12(6): 467–476.

McClintock, Martha. 1971. "Menstrual Synchrony and Suppression." *Nature* 229: 244–245.

McClintock, Martha. 1998. "Whither Menstrual Synchrony?" *Annual Review of Sex Research* 9(1): 77–95.

McCracken, Peggy. 2003. *The Curse of Eve, the Wound of the Hero: Blood, Gender, and Medieval Literature*. Philadelphia: University of Pennsylvania Press.

McFarland, Cathy, Michael Ross, and Nancy DeCourville. 1989. "Women's Theories of Menstruation and Biases in Recall of Menstrual Symptoms." *Journal of Personality and Social Psychology* 57(3): 522–531.

McLachlan, Christine, and Graham Charles Lindegger. 2012. "Queering Gender: An Exploration of the Subjective Experience of the Development of a Transgender Identity." *International Journal of Psychology* 47: 288–289.

Mohanty, Chandra. 2003. *Feminism without Borders: Decolonizing Theory, Practicing Solidarity*. Durham: Duke University Press.

Moore, Lisa Jean. 2008. *Sperm Counts: Overcome by Man's Most Precious Fluid*. New York: New York University Press.

Morgan, Robin. 1970. *Sisterhood Is Powerful.* New York: Random House.

Morgan, Robin. 1984. *Sisterhood Is Global: The International Women's Movement Anthology.* Garden City: Anchor Press/Doubleday.

Morgan, Sarah W. 2012. "Transgender Identity Development as Represented by a Group of Transgendered Adults." *Issues in Mental Health Nursing* 33(5): 301–308.

Mottax, Clifford J. 1985. "The Relative Importance of Intrinsic and Extrinsic Rewards as Determinants of Work Satisfaction." *The Sociological Quarterly* 26(3): 365–385.

Moya, Miguel, Peter Glick, Francisca Expósito, Soledad de Lemus, and Joshua Hart. 2007. " 'It's For Your Own Good': Benevolent Sexism and Women's Reactions to Protectively Justified Restrictions." *Personality and Social Psychology Bulletin* 33(10): 1421–1434.

Mutunda, Sylvester. 2006. "A Sociolinguistic Study of Politeness Strategies in the Lunda Culture." *Language, Society, and Culture* 17: 1–21.

My New Pink Button. www.mynewpinkbutton.com.

Newcomer, Laura. 2012. "Do Women's Periods Really Sync Up?" *Shape.* http://www.shape.com/lifestyle/mind-and-body/do-womens-periods-really-sync.

Nuttbrock, Larry, Andrew Rosenblum, and Rosalyne Blumenstein. 2002. "Transgender Identity Affirmation and Mental Health." *International Journal of Transgenderism* 6(4): 1–15.

Ogden, Thomas H. 1993. *The Matrix of the Mind: Object Relations and the Psychoanalytic Dialogue.* New York: Jason Aronson.

Peterson, Rachel D., Karen P. Grippo, and Stacey Tantleff-Dunn. 2008. "Empowerment and Powerlessness: A Closer Look at the Relationship between Feminism, Body Image, and Eating Disturbance." *Sex Roles* 58(9–10): 639–648.

Pfeffer, Carla A. 2008. "Bodies in Relation—Bodies in Transition: Lesbian Partners of Trans Men and Body Image." *Journal of Lesbian Studies* 12(4): 325–345.

Philipson, Ilene J. 1993. *On the Shoulders of Women: The Feminization of Psychotherapy.* New York: Guilford Press.

Preti, George, Winnifred Cutler, Celso Garcia, George Huggins, and Henry Lawley. 1986. "Human Axillary Secretions Influence Women's Menstrual Cycles: The Role of Donor Extract of Females." *Hormones and Behavior* 20(4): 474–482.

Price, Jonathan, Victoria Cole, and Guy M. Goodwin. 2009. "Emotional Side-Effects of Selective Serotonin Reuptake Inhibitors: Qualitative Study." *The British Journal of Psychiatry* 195: 211–217.

Quercia, Jacopo della. 2010, August 16. "The 7 Most Horrifying Museums on Earth." *Cracked.* http://www.cracked.com/article_18686_the-7-most-horrifying-museums-earth.html.

Quint, Chella. 2009. "Adventures in Menstruating." http://chartyourcycle. wordpress.com/zines/.

Read, Sara. 2008. "'Thy Righteousness is but a Menstrual Clout': Sanitary Practices and Prejudices in Early Modern England." *Early Modern Women* 3: 1–25.

Reading, Wiley. 2014. "My Period and Me: A Trans Guy's Guide to Menstruation." *Everyday Feminism*. http://everydayfeminism.com/2014/11/trans-guys-guide-menstruation/.

Rembeck, Gun I., Margareta M. Moller, and Ronny K. Gunnarsson. 2006. "Attitudes and Feelings towards Menstruation and Womanhood in Girls at Menarche." *Acta Paediatrica* 95(6): 707–714.

Richmond, Kate A., Theodore Burnes, and Kate Carroll. 2012. "Lost in Trans-lation: Interpreting Systems of Trauma for Transgender Clients." *Traumatology* 18(1): 45–57.

Rittenour, Christine E., and Colleen Warner Colaner. 2012. "Finding Female Fulfillment: Intersecting Role-Based and Morality-Based Identifiers of Motherhood, Feminism, and Generativity as Predictors of Women's Self-Satisfaction and Life Satisfaction." *Sex Roles* 67(5–6): 351–362.

Roberts, Tomi-Ann. 2004. "Female Trouble: The Menstrual Self-Evaluation Scale and Women's Self-Objectification." *Psychology of Women Quarterly* 28(1): 22–26.

Roberts, Tomi-Ann, and Jamie L. Goldenberg. 2007. "Wrestling with Nature: An Existential Perspective on the Body and Gender in Self-Conscious Emotions." In *The Self-Conscious Emotions: Theory and Research*, edited by Jessica L. Tracy, Richard W. Robins, and June Price Tangney, 389–406. New York: Guilford Press.

Roberts, Tomi-Ann, and Patricia Waters. 2004. "Self-Objectification and That 'Not So Fresh Feeling': Feminist Therapeutic Interventions for Healthy Female Embodiment." *Women & Therapy* 27(3–4): 5–21.

Roscigno, Vincent J., and Randy Hodson. 2004. "The Organizational and Social Foundations of Worker Resistance." *American Sociological Review* 69(1): 14–39.

Rose, Jennifer Gorman, Joan C. Chrisler, and Samantha Couture. 2008. "Young Women's Attitudes toward Continuous Use of Oral Contraceptives: The Effect of Priming Positive Attitudes toward Menstruation on Women's Willingness to Suppress Menstruation. *Health Care for Women International* 29(7): 688–701.

Rosewarne, Lauren. 2012. *Periods in Pop Culture: Menstruation in Film and Television*. New York: Lexington Books.

Ruddick-Sunstein, Ellyn. 2014, June 9. "Women Take to the Streets Wearing Menstrual Blood Stains." *Beautiful/Decay*. http://beautifuldecay. com/2014/06/09/women-take-streets-wearing-menstrual-blood-stains/.

Russell, Michael, Genevieve Switz, and Kate Thompson. 1980. "Olfactory Influences on the Human Menstrual Cycle." *Pharmacology, Biochemistry, & Behaviour* 13(5): 737–738.

Sallans, Ryan K. 2012. "Serving the Transgender Community." *Contemporary Sexuality* 46(9): 1–5.

Sangre Menstrual. 2009. *Manifesto por la Visibilidad de la Regla.* http://sangremenstrual.wordpress.com/2009/05/17/manifiesto-por-la-visibilidad-de-la-regla/.

Sangre Menstrual. 2010. "Una Selección de Imágenes de la Performance del Colectivo Sangre Menstrual por las Calles de Madrid en Marzo de 2010." http://issuu.com/olmo/docs/sangre_menstrual_performance.

Santer, Miriam, Sally Wyke, and Pam Warner. 2008. "Women's Management of Menstrual Symptoms: Findings from a Postal Survey and Qualitative Interviews." *Social Science & Medicine* 66(2): 276–288.

Sarachild, Kathie. 1975. *Feminist Revolution.* New York: Random House.

Saul, Heather. 2015. "Menstruation-Themed Photo Series Artist 'Censored' by Instagram Says Images Are to Demystify Taboos around Periods." *The Independent.* http://www.independent.co.uk/arts-entertainment/art/menstruationthemed-photo-series-artist-censored-by-instagram-says-images-are-to-demystify-taboos-around-periods-10144331.html.

Schank, Jeffrey. 2000. "Menstrual-Cycle Variability and Measurement: Further Cause for Doubt." *Psychoneuroendocrinology* 25(8): 837–847.

Schank, Jeffrey. 2001. "Menstrual-Cycle Synchrony: Problems and New Directions for Research." *Journal of Comparative Psychology* 115(1): 3–15.

Schank, Jeffrey. 2002. "A Multitude of Errors in Menstrual-Synchrony Research: Replies to Weller and Weller (2002) and Graham (2002)." *Journal of Comparative Psychology* 116(3): 319–322.

Schank, Jeffrey. 2006. "Do Human Menstrual-Cycle Pheromones Exist?" *Human Nature* 17(4): 448–470.

Schick, Vanessa R., Alyssa N. Zucker, and Laina Y. Bay-Cheng. 2008. "Safer, Better Sex through Feminism: The Role of Feminist Ideology in Women's Sexual Well-Being." *Psychology of Women Quarterly* 32(3): 225–232.

Schiff, Bob. 2010. "Komodo Island Voyage." *Hamptons.* http://www.hamptons.com/Lifestyle//Main-Articles/12199/Komodo-Island-Voyage.html?sectionName=Outdoors-And-Fitness&columnName=Main-Articles&articleID=12199#.UkRazT-JKSp.

Schleifer, David. 2006. "Make Me Feel Mighty Real: Gay Female-to-Male Transgenderists Negotiating Sex, Gender, and Sexuality." *Sexualities* 9(1): 57–75.

Schooler, Deborah, Monique Ward, Ann Merriwether, and Allison Caruthers. 2005. "Cycles of Shame: Menstrual Shame, Body Shame, and Sexual Decision-Making." *Journal of Sex Research* 42(4): 324–334.

Seed, David. 1985. "The Narrative Method of Dracula." *Nineteenth-Century Fiction* 40(1): 61–75.

Semonche, John E. 2007. *Censoring Sex: A Historical Journey through American Media*. Lanham: Rowman & Littlefield.

Sennett, Richard. 2011. *The Corrosion of Character: The Personal Consequences of Work in the New Capitalism*. New York: W.W. Norton & Company.

Shuttle, Penelope, and Peter Redgrove. 1988. *The Wise Wound: The Myths, Realities, and Meanings of Menstruation*. New York: Grove Press.

Simon, Bernd, and Bert Klandermans. 2001. "Politicized Collective Identity: A Social Psychological Analysis." *American Psychologist* 56(4): 319–331.

Snow, David, Burke Rochford Jr., Steven Worden, Robert Benford. 1986. "Frame Alignment Processes, Micromobilization, and Movement Participation." *American Sociological Review* 51(4): 464–481.

Society for Menstrual Cycle Research. *Re:Cycling*. http://menstruationresearch.org/blog.

Solanas, Valerie. 1996. *SCUM Manifesto*. San Francisco: AK Press.

Stake, Jayne E. 2007. "Predictors of Change in Feminist Activism through Women's and Gender Studies Classes." *Sex Roles* 57: 43–54.

Stake, Jayne E., and Frances L. Hoffmann. 2000. "Putting Feminist Pedagogy to the Test: The Experience of Women's Studies from Student and Teacher Perspectives." *Psychology of Women Quarterly* 24: 30–38.

Stake, Jayne E., Laurie Roades, Suzanna Rose, Lisa Ellis, and Carolyn West. 1994. "The Women's Studies Experience: Impetus for Feminist Activism." *Psychology of Women Quarterly* 18(1): 17–24.

Stern, Kathleen, and Martha McClintock. 1998. "Regulation of Ovulation by Human Pheromones." *Nature* 392: 177–179.

Strassmann, Beverly. 1997. "The Biology of Menstruation in *Homo sapiens*: Total Lifetime Menses, Fecundity, and Nonsynchrony in a Natural-Fertility Population." *Current Anthropology* 38(1): 123–129.

Strassmann, Beverly. 1999. "Menstrual Synchrony Pheromones: Cause for Doubt." *Human Reproduction* 14(3): 579–580.

Stryker, Susan, Paisley Currah, and Lisa Jean Moore. 2008. "Introduction: Trans-, trans, or transgender?" *WSQ* 36(3–4): 11–22.

Stubbs, Margaret L., and Daryl Costos. 2004. "Negative Attitudes toward Menstruation: Implications for Disconnection within Girls and between Women." *Women & Therapy* 27(3–4): 37–54.

Swim, Janet K., and Laurie L. Cohen. 1997. "Overt, Covert, and Subtle Sexism: A Comparison between the Attitudes toward Women and Modern Sexism Scales." *Psychology of Women Quarterly* 21(1): 103–118.

Szymanski, Dawn M., and Gina P. Owens. 2009. "Group-Level Coping as a Moderator between Heterosexism and Sexism and Psychological Distress in Sexual Minority Women." *Psychology of Women Quarterly* 33(2): 197–205.

"10 Most Bizarre Museums." 2007, June 1. *Oddee*. http://www.oddee.com/item_86041.aspx.

Thornton, Leslie-Jean. 2013. "'Time of the Month' on Twitter: Taboo, Stereotype, and Bonding in a No-Holds-Barred Public Arena." *Sex Roles* 68(1–2): 41–54.

Tickner, Lisa. 1987. "The Body Politic: Female Sexuality and Women Artists since 1970." In *Looking On: Images of Femininity in the Visual Arts and Media*, edited by Rosemary Betterton, 235–253. London: Pandora.

Tiggemann, Marika, and Christine Lewis. 2004. "Attitudes toward Women's Body Hair: Relationship with Disgust Sensitivity." *Psychology of Women Quarterly* 28(4): 381–387.

Tilden, Emma. 2014. "Let's Think Period Positive and Celebrate." *Bust*. http://bust.com/lets-think-period-positive-and-celebrate.html.

Tone, Andrea. 1996. "Contraceptive Consumers: Gender and the Political Economy of Birth Control in the 1930s." *Journal of Social History* 29(3): 485–506.

Trevathan, Wenda, Mary Burleson, and Larry Gregory. 1993. "No Evidence for Menstrual Synchrony in Lesbian Couples." *Psychoneuroendocrinology* 18(5–6): 425–435.

Turke, Paul. 1984. "Effects of Ovulatory Concealment and Synchrony on Protohominid Mating Systems and Parental Roles." *Ethology and Sociobiology* 5(1): 33–44.

Umeora, Ouj, and Ve Egwuatu. 2008. "Age at Menarche and the Menstrual Pattern of Igbo Women of Southeast Nigeria." *African Journal of Reproductive Health* 12(1): 90–95.

Uskul, Ayse. 2004. "Women's Menarche Stories from a Multicultural Sample." *Social Science & Medicine* 59(4): 667–679.

Ussher, Jane M., and Janette Perz. 2008. "Empathy, Egalitarianism, and Emotion Work in the Relational Negotiation of PMS: The Experience of Women in Lesbian Relationships." *Feminism & Psychology* 18(1): 87–111.

Vidal, John. 2008, June 11. "The Terrifying Truth about Komodo Dragons." *The Guardian*. http://www.theguardian.com/world/2008/jun/12/indonesia.

Wagner, James. 2010, December 17. "Censorship and Homophobia, AIDS, Sex, Art, Religion." http://jameswagner.com/2010/12/censorship.html.

Walpole, Matthew J., and Harold J. Goodwin. 2000. "Local Economic Impacts of Dragon Tourism in Indonesia." *Annals of Tourism Research* 27(3): 559–576.

Wark, Jayne. 2006. *Radical Gestures: Feminism and Performance Art in North America*. Montreal: McGill-Queens University Press.

Webber, Michelle. 2005. "'Don't Be So Feminist': Exploring Student Resistance to Feminist Approaches in a Canadian University." *Women's Studies International Forum* 28: 181–194.

Weller, Aron, and Leonard Weller. 1992. "Menstrual Synchrony in Female Couples." *Psychoneuroendocrinology* 17(2–3): 171–177.

Weller, Aron, and Leonard Weller. 1993a. "Human Menstrual Synchrony: A Critical Assessment." *Neuroscience & Biobehavioral Reviews* 17(4): 427–439.

Weller, Aron, and Leonard Weller. 1993b. "Menstrual Synchrony between Mothers and Daughters and between Roommates." *Physiology & Behavior* 53(5): 943–949.

Weller, Aron, and Leonard Weller. 1995a. Examination of Menstrual Synchrony among Women Basketball Players." *Psychoneuroendocrinology* 20(6): 613–622.

Weller, Aron, and Leonard Weller. 1995b. "The Impact of Social Interaction Factors on Menstrual Synchrony in the Workplace." *Psychoneuroendocrinology* 20(1): 21–31.

Weller, Aron, and Leonard Weller. 1998. "Prolonged and Very Intensive Contact May Not Be Conducive to Menstrual Synchrony." *Psychoneuroendocrinology* 23(1): 19–32.

Weller, Aron, and Leonard Weller. 2002a. "Menstrual Irregularity and Menstrual Symptoms." *Behavioral Medicine* 27(4): 173–178.

Weller, Aron, and Leonard Weller. 2002b. "Menstrual Synchrony Can Be Assessed, Inherent Cycle Variability Notwithstanding: Commentary on Schank (2001)." *Journal of Comparative Psychology* 116(3): 316–318.

Weller, Leonard, and Aron Weller. 1995c. "Menstrual Synchrony: Agenda for Future Research." *Psychoneuroendocrinology* 20(4): 377–383.

Weller, Leonard, and Aron Weller. 1997. "Menstrual Variability and the Measurement of Menstrual Synchrony." *Psychoneuroendocrinology* 22(2): 115–128.

Weller, Leonard, and Aron Weller. 2002. "Menstrual Synchrony and Cycle Variability: A Reply to Schank (2000)." *Psychoneuroendocrinology* 27(4): 519–526.

Weller, Leonard, Aron Weller, and Ohela Avinir. 1995. "Menstrual Synchrony: Only in Roommates Who Are Close Friends?" *Physiology & Behavior* 58(5): 883–889.

Weller, Leonard, Aron Weller, and Shoshana Roizman. 1999. "Human Menstrual Synchrony in Families and among Close Friends: Examining the Importance of Mutual Exposure." *Journal of Comparative Psychology* 113(3): 261–268.

Weller, Leonard, Aron Weller, Hagit Koresh-Kamin, and Rivi Ben-Shoshan. 1999. "Menstrual Synchrony in a Sample of Working Women." *Psychoneuroendocrinology* 24(4): 449–459.

Wilson, Clyde. 1992. "A Critical Review of Menstrual Synchrony Research." *Psychoneuroendocrinology* 17(6): 565–591.

Wilson, Clyde, Sarah Kiefhaber, and Virginia Gravel. 1991. "Two Studies of Menstrual Synchrony: Negative Results." *Psychoneuroendocrinology* 16(4): 353–359.

White, Lisandra Rodriguez. 2013. "The Function of Ethnicity, Income Level, and Menstrual Taboos in Postmenarcheal Adolescents' Understanding of Menarche and Menstruation." *Sex Roles* 68(1–2): 65–76.

Wister, Joseph Albert, Margaret L. Stubbs, and Chaquica Shipman. 2013. "Mentioning Menstruation: A Stereotype Threat That Diminishes Cognition?" *Sex Roles* 68(1–2): 19–31.

Yalom, Marilyn. 1997. *A History of the Breast.* New York: Knopf.

Yang, Zhengwei, and Jeffrey Schank. 2006. "Women Do Not Synchronize Their Menstrual Cycles." *Human Nature* 17(4): 433–447.

Yoder, Janice, Ann Tobias, and Andrea Snell. 2011. "When Declaring 'I Am a Feminist' Matters: Labeling Is Linked to Activism." *Sex Roles* 64(1–2): 9–18.

Young, Iris Marion. 1997. "Menstrual Meditations." In *On Female Body Experience: Throwing Like a Girl and Other Essays*, edited by Iris Marion Young, 97–122. New York: Oxford University Press.

Ziomkiewicz, Anna. 2006. "Menstrual Synchrony: Fact or Artifact?" *Human Nature* 17(4): 419–432.

Index